Mexico by Erwin Fieger

Mexico
by
Erwin Fieger

Universe Books

© 1973 by Accidentia Druck-
und Verlags-GmbH,
Düsseldorf
© 1973 for the photographs
for all countries in the
International Copyright
Union by Erwin Fieger

Foreword: Rosa Elena Luján
Text: Marianne Greenwood
All rights reserved.
Offset reproductions in
four colors in format of
24 x 36 mm.: Helmut Peter
Conrad KG, Solingen-Wald

Production:
Busche, Dortmund
Conception and design:
Erwin Fieger
LC number: 74-83563
ISBN 0-87663-190-1
Printed in West Germany

Rosa Elena Luján, 57, born in Progreso, Yucatán, Mexico, was the eleventh child of a family of twelve children. Having studied both in Mexico and in the United States, she specialized in translating work in the languages of these countries. She married Carlos Montes de Oca, a Mexican industrialist, deceased in 1960, from whom she has two daughters, Rosa Elena and Maria Eugenia; also a grandchild, Irene, by her first daughter. In 1953, she was called upon to translate the motion picture script of "The Rebellion of the Hanged," which had been written by Hal Croves, representative of the author, B. Traven.

While being introduced to Mr. Croves, there came to her memory another introduction which had taken place many years before, in 1936. "Meet Torsvan, photographer," her Scandinavian friends Helga Larsen and Bodil Christensen had said while introducing to her the same man she now had in front of her.

After this surprise re-encounter Rosa Elena Luján and Hal Croves, alias B. Traven, became close friends and collaborators, but she was far from knowing that the man

Marianne Greenwood. Writer and photographer. Born Marianne Hederstrom in Gallivaare, Sweden, April 5th, 1926.

After spending her childhood in Lapland, studied at the Art Academy in Stockholm. Lived in France – Paris and Antibes – 1950–1960, travelling extensively in Europe. Continuous travels through North, Middle, and South America 1961–1973.

Photographic Publications: (Books)
"Vignette pour les vignerons," text by Jacques Prévert, drawings by Françoise Gilot, Paris 1953. "Picasso au Musée d'Antibes," text by André Verdet, Paris 1954. "Svarta tjurar," text by Evert Taube, Stockholm 1958. "Picasso in Antibes," text by Dor de la Souchère, New York 1960. "Återkomst," text by Evert Taube, Stockholm 1961. "Land of the Mayas, Yesterday and Today," text by Carleton Beals, 1967. "Land of the Incas," text by Carleton Beals,

Erwin Fieger, born in 1928, in Töplei, Czechoslovakia. Training as a graphic designer at the Staatliche Akademie der Bildenden Künste (State Academy of Fine Arts), in Stuttgart/Germany. Now free-lance photographer in Düsseldorf. From 1957 to 1962, occasionally occupied with color photography, since 1962 active photographer. Pioneer of modern color photography, publication of books and calendars. Designer and coauthor of the exhibition and photo book "Magic with the colour camera" (photokina, Cologne, and Biennale Venice, 1960). In 1962, photo report "London – city of any dream." In 1962, one-man exhibition of 70 large-size color pictures. In 1963, photo report "Grand Prix." In 1963/64, feature report "Deutsche Lufthansa." Guiding conception for airline advertising with exclusive use of color photos. 1966: Designer and coauthor of the exhibition "Farbige Essays" (photokina, Cologne). In 1968, photo-

she was working for was really the world-famous writer, B. Traven.

She has translated seven Traven books into Spanish. The other ones had already been translated by Esperanza Lopez Mateos, sister of Mexico's ex-president.
In addition to translating, Señora Luján writes newspaper articles, cinema scripts and short stories.
She married B. Traven Torsvan in 1957 in the United States of America.

Since his death in 1969, she has continued working on new editions and on everything relating to the works of B. Traven.

New York 1973. "The Navajos," text by Raymond Friday Locke, Los Angeles 1973.

Various small art books in France, co-photographer for a book about the sculptures by Germaine Richier, Galerie Creuzevault, Paris, plus many articles in French and Swedish magazines like VI and Konstrevy.

Photographic:
Illustrations for various articles in Mankind Magazine published in the beginning of 1970 and the end of 1969, plus 1971, 1972 and 1973.
Text for articles about the Huichole-Indians, and Devil's Islands, French Guiana, plus photos.

graphic report "13 Photo-Essays" (was awarded the Prix Nadar in Paris, in 1969).
In 1970, photographic design of the theme "Gardens of Music," German pavilion of the World's Fair in Osaka.
In 1971, photo report "Japan Sunrise Islands" (was in 1973 awarded the silver medal at the 3rd Biennale in Jerusalem).
In 1972, Olympic photographic reports "Sapporo 1972," "München 1972." The successful attempt of representing the Olympic Winter and Summer Games by means of pictures shot mainly by a photographer (was in 1973 awarded the gold medal by the Art Directors Club of Germany).

Rosa Elena Luján

When Erwin Fieger visited me in my Mexico City home together with a mutual friend, I noticed he was carrying a large book under his arm; and whenever I see someone with a book or a newspaper, I get an impulse to snatch it away and read it immediately.

I always did this when my husband came home from the post office with a parcel, and I knew instantly that it was a new edition of one of his books; another volume by "B. Traven."

In a matter of seconds, I had torn the wrappings off with the help of fingernails, teeth and scissors while he stood there feigning anger at my behaviour.

"It's from Germany, darling," I said. "A very handsome edition of 'The Death Ship.'"

"East or West?," he would ask.

"West. But I thought it would be 'The Treasure of the Sierra Madre' from Italy. It's due, you know."

This time, though, I acted very differently in the presence of my guests. Although Mr. Fieger had placed on a table before him his beautiful book on Japan and I was burning to see the photographs of which I had heard so much, I tried to act politely and asked whether he cared for a drink: "Would you like a tequila with lemon and salt? Or perhaps you prefer to taste real mezcal from the Sierra of Oaxaca? A friend of mine just brought me a jug of the very best."

Still restraining myself, I then asked very casually, "May I see the book?"

"Of course, Mrs. Traven, it is for you."

While my other guest, as if reading my mind, took him aside to show him some paintings collected by my husband and myself during our many years together, as well as some photographs done by famous photographers, such as Weston (from whom Traven took lessons), Tina Modotti, Alvarez Bravo, Gabriel Figueroa and others, I had my first opportunity to examine Erwin Fieger's photographic work.

Opening that book was like opening a door to dreams. His highly artistic concept and great technique magnificently reproduced therein would take many words to describe. Rather, Fieger's photographs are not only to be seen but to be felt and to be lived. He first captures one by entrancement, then he makes one live them. Yes, I have the feeling that this truly describes it, whether he realizes it or not. His work on Mexico has a special significance for me. Forms and textures are familiar. And apart from the natural emotion one feels when contemplating a work of art, these photographs bring back warm memories of travels with my husband, and although this is not a book of travel, mind you – definitely not – nor is it a record of one or of many trips to Mexico, it's a book which shows that Erwin Fieger, the artist, was here with a camera at the service of his talent and sensibility.

When Traven arrived in the early twenties, he roamed the Republic not only with his typewriter, but also with his camera, a big, bulky, box-shaped affair.

Photography was a passion with him although he personally disliked being photographed. Certain inhabitants of the States of Puebla and Chiapas also do not like to be photographed and they reject any attempt to do so but for altogether different reasons. They believe that part of the soul is "robbed" by the image, so that when one dies the soul is not complete to accompany one into the new experience.

Mexico is a country for spacious wanderings. A frontier of almost two thousand miles joins it to the north with the United States of America and it is encompassed within more than six thousand miles of seaboard between the Pacific and Atlantic oceans with a land extension of about 770,000 square miles.

I wish I had been with Traven when he explored much of this, I wish I had shared with him all of his adventures, those at sea, or those among the peasants. I wish I had accompanied him on his archeological expeditions looking for hidden pyramids and well-guarded tombs; I wish I could have experienced the drama of the mahogany camps in the jungle of Chiapas, a state in the Southeast bordering Guatemala, which was to become his favourite. Six related novels, a book of tropical travel profusely illustrated with photographs taken by him and many short stories were inspired by this region of Mexico.

In those times it was not easy to develop pictures in the jungle with jaguars, ocelots (Mexican leopards), snakes and an assortment of insects as curious visitors. But he could not afford to leave the place without making sure that his pictures were successful as another trip to the same place meant another expedition on horseback while his photographic equipment was carried by mule.

I like to look at his old cameras; those that went with him to the jungle, and the darkroom candle lamps; developing trays, thermometers, yes even unused packages of developer and fixing powders I have kept. Also leftover boxes of printing paper. These things, unimportant in themselves, recall the beautiful times we spent together.

I can imagine him asking his Indian guide to bring him water, very clean and fresh from a nearby stream, for the developing process. The water might not have come from a stream but from a river, perhaps as Traven himself describes it even from "the imposing, powerful, mysterious Usumacinta where rose-colored birds circle inquisitively around. Perceiving no danger, they spiral in wide arcs towards the sandy banks of the majestic river, finally glide down, walking on their long thin legs as if on stilts leisurely into the slowly flowing water, and begin, rather solemnly, to fish."

In the early days he used German cameras; later he had American makes. The last one he used was Japanese, which was lost somewhere in Mazatlán.

He never bought costly cameras or typewriters; all his equipment was unfailingly modest, except for one very fine lens which he treasured.

Years later, when I came into his life, we went to many places all over Mexico because of his insatiable thirst for travel.

Most of his gifts to me or to our daughters were short or long trips, depending on what he could afford at the time.

Often I would see him take a mango or a peach from a box of fruit like those expressed so vividly in Fieger's work.

The photographer reveals himself as a genuine colorist. These are very powerful prints in their apparent simplicity. But isn't simplicity the secret of artistic work? The beauty of colour is latent, and how much technique is needed and what aid from an experienced printer is required for a perfect reproduction? I am not an expert on these matters.

Changing from one theme to another, Fieger manages to magnetize us into the nets of the fishermen in the shallow waters of Lake Pátzcuaro in Michoacán . . . are these nets the wings of a giant butterfly? Again, we are as securely trapped as the unique white fish of that lake which the peaceful fishermen catch amid surroundings of exuberant vegetation.

The artist's ideal is completely fulfilled here; to entrance the spectator with his magic spell. In pre-Columbian times this region was part of the Tarascan nation and the Indians still speak the Tarascan language, using Spanish only to trade with the mestizos.

But why should we continue to call them Indians? All is Mexican; whether Indians, Mestizos and Creoles. Mexico is also its naturalized citizens who choose to become so.

On the shores of this lake stands the town of Janitzio. Here a cult to the dead strongly prevails. My husband and I liked to go there on November 2, día de muertos (All Souls Day). On the previous night, the inhabitants prepare ofrendas (offerings) for their dead relatives, of food, fruits, sugar-coated sweetmeats and water. Yes, water! because the dead not only must eat but also quench their thirst from glasses which are filled to the brim and the level of which the following morning has been observed to descend an inch or so! All artistically decorated with fresh flowers or a paper variety placed over tablecloths of curiously cut paper. It is a night-long wake with which they accompany their relatives in the spirit by the flickering light of hundreds of candles against the darkness of the night which gives it a truly ghostly setting. In all surrounding townships similar ceremonies are taking place in the cemeteries with people praying and singing the night through. The next day they will consume what the dead have left of that wonderful repast.

However, as so many tourists from Mexico and abroad are attracted to the spectacle, the people of Janitzio, in order to safeguard their ancient traditions, have decided to celebrate the ceremony at another undisclosed time. Tarascans are very close to nature in their artistic expression. In their view, men are men, animals are animals, and flowers are such. Did Fieger know that this realism predominates there or did he just sense it? Because his photographs do show us Michoacán in all its reality, in all its truth.

Routine daily life of people in the big cities or small towns: the face of a baby, the organ-grinder, and such are so actively pictured. Moving shapes thrust in every direction, be they men or animals. Faces hardly perceptible in deep shadow. A poor old couple selling paper flowers expresses the dignity and kindness of old age.

The gigantic growth of Mexico City with all its contrasts, with its content of one fifth of the population of the country and where the greatest economic activity takes place makes of it, like so many other large urban concentrations, an island of luxury surrounded by a sea of misery as evidenced by the so-called "lost cities" which have grown on its outskirts.

In contrast, Fieger gives us his interpretation of the quietness of the countryside. Thickets of bushes and shrubs, plants beginning their life, and every shade of greenery with red, black and brown soil.

There is majestic splendour in Fieger's landscapes and views. Places which we have seen a dozen times acquire a different dimension from his gifted and aesthetic vision. Great observer of nature that he is, combined with his creative spirit, he conveys color – color which he has turned into pure light – or is it the other way around, light which he has alchemized into color? . . . because a poet will describe the world to us the way he sees it.

The repetition of a theme carried to an excess shows his genuine greatness, rigour, purity, severity.

His photographs of the devout strike one deeply, the expressions, attitudes.

One breathes mysticism in the air.

As their ancestors did, long before the Spaniards came, these people have always had a deep respect for the unknown, for the magic power of the occult. Their existence revolves about the faith and observance of the ancient rites, which are a curious mixture of Christianity and the old beliefs.

To this day they worship both the new god of the conquerors and the autoch-thonous deities. We once visited a Catholic church in the vicinity of Amecameca where we were surprised to see a pre-Columbian deity on the altar accompanying images of the Christ, the Virgin and several Saints. On inquiring of the incumbent priest why he had permitted this apparently unorthodox situation, he told us that he had to yield to popular request as the entire population threatened never to set foot again in his church unless at least one of their local gods was on hand!

In their religious observances they like to represent legendary or historical events. These pageants usually take place during Holy Week when battles between Moors and Christians, Cortes and Cuauhtémoc, and the French intervention are the order of the day.

However, the most important religious celebration is on December 12 which is dedicated to our Lady of Guadalupe. Multitudes go to the Basílica which was built in her honour and where she is serenaded, revered and regaled by several days of native dances.

It is interesting to observe that their ancestors made pilgrimages exactly to the same place and in the same month long before the Conquest, only that in those times they were paying homage to the mother-goddess Tonantzin!

To impose the new religion on the conquered people, the Spaniards built a Christian monument atop all local temples and places of worship.

The main Catholic monument in Mexico is the cathedral, the first to be built in this continent and which was begun in 1573 on the ruins of the great Aztec Teocalli, using part of the same material of the original temple and particularly the carved stones thereof.

Fieger presents us with an almost allegorical duplicate vision of the cathedral, employing repetitive reflections which hover halo-like.

Strolling around with my husband was a real treat. Never tired, always springy and curious to see new things, he always had a story to tell in his fascinating way about every place we saw, whether it might be the volcanoes or a pyramid.

I shall never forget the day we climbed the Tepoztlán pyramid for the worship of the the god of pulque, a fermented beverage made from the maguey plant (agave). It was a real effort to climb this steep rock and I was exhausted, but the magnificent view from the top, incomparable in its scope and majesty dominating the Cuernavaca valley, was reward enough for our efforts. On our return to the small hotel where we were staying, all I wanted was a good rest. Not so my husband; he was thirsty but there was no appropriate beverage at the place, so he still walked quite a number of blocks to get it and drink to the health of the god Tepoztecátl in whose honour the pyramid was built. I am still sorry I was so tired

I could not please them both and I hope this god does not know that my husband was more than twenty-five years my senior, because then I will not only be sorry, but also ashamed, terribly ashamed!

I am Mexican, born in Yucatán in a house by the beach of the small port of Progreso. But I never found a place in this country that I could show that "foreigner" husband of mine, which he did not already know much better than I.

By now you have guessed that I, as a Maya, not only burn copal (incense) to the old gods Quetzalcóatl-Kukulkán and Chac (the rain god) but that most of it is consumed to the memory of Traven.

Fieger displays the strength and plastic perfection found in Mayan creations. The archeological reliefs, rendered in blue, are sublime, almost sacred.

Mexico is a country that prevails on the photographer to bring out all his creative ambitions and aesthetic ideals, and Erwin Fieger has done so. This book is the proof.

Rosa Elena Luján
México, D.F., May 28, 1973

Marianne Greenwood

It was a day in autumn many years ago, in London.
"You are always talking about Mexico!" My friend Fritz Lang, the great film-producer and a turbulent man of genius to boot, glared at me angrily, "I'll show you how little you understand!"
Taxi to the British Museum. Up the stairs. In.
"Close your eyes!" he commanded. – "You may on no account open them till I tell you to. Come!"
He pushed me along energetically. For days and nights, it seemed, we stumbled through the dark periods of history, the world and all its continents, through one single infinite night, before Fritz took my arm in a steely grip and shouted:
"Open your eyes!"
There, solitary on its pedestal, stood a glimmering object.
I stared, dazzled by the light streaming from it. The thing stared back with such intensity that I was forced to avert my gaze. The glare from the empty sockets continued to scorch me. This sublime object was a life-size cranium of rock crystal, of Mixteca or Aztec manufacture.
The intense concentration of light and reflexes in the veins of the crystal conveyed the impression that the invisible brain was producing thoughts.

The cranium lived. Laughed, spoke, existed!
"Well!" Fritz was not the man to leave anything half done. – "What do you understand?"
I was speechless. More confused than ever.
"The human being!" shouted Fritz. – "The human being, don't you understand that! Mexico is the Mexican! The person and his thoughts. The individual! Landscape is the one who regards it, landscape is a state of soul. You can never understand Mexico until you have understood every one of the inhabitants. Living or dead!"
Why, in the art of Old Mexico, did death and the human skull play such a prominent rôle?
"While the skins of certain animals, the feathers of certain birds, or perfect shells may be more beautiful than the human body or skin, there is nothing in Nature so perfect as the human skull. In the old cultures of Mexico aesthetic values had great importance. Nor may it be forgotten that there was no such thing as a dead object, everything was considered to possess a soul and to have moral value."
(José Pijoan's explanation in his "Summa Artis.")
It is not only in Mexican art that we find death everywhere present, but also in the daily

life of the people, today as yesterday. Apart from its being a phase in the process of life and rebirth, innumerable other explanations are conceivable.

The Mexicans themselves are so incredibly alive that it is almost embarrassing for a life-weary old European. Mexico gives us a lesson in the art of living. And, further to enhance the feeling of life and the slenderness of the thread that binds us to it, death is always, almost palpably, present. He is a friend that is invited to the feast. It is not only in Diego Rivera's fresco paintings that Dame Sorrow in a black lace dress with a skeleton painted on it walks at the head of the carnival procession; and the Mexican children play with dangling toy skeletons and suck sugar crania where the involutions of the brain are ornamentally spread on in chocolate icing. The price of living in this dramatic country is quite evidently death.

Grinning, humoristic, human, our Mexican continues to be a part of life itself.

There is so much to see in Mexico that it is enough to fill one's eyes for the rest of one's life. Mexico is a country of great contradictions and great dimensions. Here is everything, but more of every-thing: it is blacker, whiter, the colours are gaudier, it is more beautiful, more cruel, grief here is more harrowing, joy more delirious. Mexico is exuberantly rich and frighteningly sterile, passionately wild and immoderately lovely.

The Mexican himself, on the surface carefree but full of complexes and weighed upon by a bloody history, is a being more spiritual than physical. He is romantic to the point of sentimentality, reckless, sometimes comically touching, always noble and incredibly handsome.

One may fall in love with a country, and with an incurable, passionate love I am bound to Mexico. First of all it is the country itself, then I love the Mexican men, no, the children! and then the women, and finally the Mexican dogs, the donkeys in Mexico, the sun – Mexico's hot sun, the mariachi music, the pigs, the ants on the paths of Mexico, the parrots in the trees of the Mexican jungle, and well – since I love people – I love the tourists in Mexico!

Everyone looks for and finds his own Mexico, unique and unlike anyone else's. But no one can visit this country without being deeply affected. Enchanted, embittered, annihilated, afraid but delighted. One feels helplessly drawn into an embrace that is as ravishing and at the same time as terrifying as a night in Chiapas' jungle, the forest that never sleeps. Nothing is so fascinating as a night in the jungle with its mystique: the somehow ubiquitous murmuring from animals you do not see, the sharp but indefinable sounds of plants eating animals, wild beast devouring wild beast, animals eating plants. One feels the death agony, the death struggle, the feeling of lust and treacherous embrace, and one knows that a thousand eyes are staring at one while one is drawn deeper and deeper into the unknown. The smell of wild beasts is palpable, and is blended with the perfume of orchid and mould. The call of the tropical birds – at once frightful, delightful, hesitating and shy, viciously raucous, enticing and lisping – fills every eventual pause in the jungle concert.

Palenque, oh Palenque! Night has fallen over Palenque's temple ruins. We are sitting, a group of people from the world's great family, on the topmost step of the Palace and watching one constellation after the other appear in a deep blue night sky. The ensnaring, chokingly moist jungle, that for centuries has taken possession of every-thing, envelops us like a cloak. The sumptuously clad lords on the stucco fresco stand in line behind us, and their mysterious presence enhances the mood of unreality. In the streaming moonlight, the pyramids of the temple buildings seem like dream pictures on the point of dissolving, to merge into the black rain-forest and vanish into the recesses of history as mysteriously and without trace as their builders, and without giving us the clue we need final-ly to interpret their message. "Scientists consider that the pyramidal form acts like a magnet to, or collector of, natural radiation. All natural forces are also collected and active in each one of us," says Moises Morales, a noble-minded Mexican from the high plateau of the Aztecs but dedicated for life and eternity to Maya. He is Palenque's "soul" and the friend of the Lacandon, the last Mayas. Moises has knowledge. Moises loves. He gives his knowledge with love and a good spice of humour into the bargain. "The great man whose bones rested in 'The Temple with the Inscriptions' just opposite doubtless knew of these truths. He had the pyramid built during his life-time and arranged for his magnificent sepulchre for his eternal rest — without forgetting a channel to the fresh air so that he could breathe, or perhaps send communications to the outside world! There he lay, guarded by the Nine Lords of the Night in Mayan mythology, as undisturbed as an Egyptian Pharaoh, until 20 years ago, when a fellow named Alberto Ruz found him and opened the tomb. However, before anyone could pose a single question the mysterious king was transformed into vermilion dust and a heap of jade ornaments."

Who was he, this ruler of Palenque, do we find him on any of the weathered frescoes, do any of the hieroglyphs tell us about him? Was he perhaps the noble prince on "The Beautiful Relief," the "Relieve Hermoso" of which Count Frederick Waldeck made a drawing at the beginning of last century, though the original has since been completely effaced by time and the all-devouring rain-forest? Like a high-born Indian prince from a tale in the Arabian Nights he sits on a throne borne by two roaring jaguars and holds court. "Listen to me!" says his gesture. We listen. We hear nothing. We understand nothing. His whole appearance is witty and refined; he carries no weapons, nor is his countenance covered by any mask of religious significance. On his head wave light feathers. He is evidently a learned man and a product of an incredibly cultivated community.

What was Palenque, so unlike all other Mayan cities? A cultural and artistic centre? A metropolis for magic and occult powers? For astrology? A winter residence for kings, a Mayan Susa? Or a Mayan Olympus? A counterpart to the equally mysterious Teotihuacán, the sacred city in Mexico City's valley, "where the serpent miraculously learned to fly" – that is to say, where by cultivating his soul man attained the right to be regarded as a celestial being, and where death was only an awakening from the dream of life and the beginning of an eternal life as god! Thus a burial place! A sacred cemetery with mausoleums! We sit in silence and look at the stars, each lost in unspoken musings and guesses. Venus is shining like a sun.

"In contradistinction to other old civilizations the Mayans knew that the evening and the morning star were one and the same celestial body – Venus! However, the secrets of the cult of Venus were only for the initiated priests and scientists. They had a deep knowledge of cosmology, mathematics and other sciences…" begins Enrique, an erudite Palencophile whose studies keep him constantly travelling from one place to another, lost in the historical labyrinth of his country, which has neither entrance nor exit. "They had a more accurate calendar than we do," he goes on. – "What of such importance does astronomy do now? It was so important for the ancient Mayans that, as we know, an astronomical congress was held in Copán in 503 A.D. The result is engraved on a stone altar there."

"In order to get maize to grow in this tropical jungle the priests had to have a deep knowledge of astronomy, as the planting of maize is not conditioned by the seasons but depends on the rainy periods which are in their turn dependent on the shifting influence of the moon. The Lacandon still sow their maize according to the old Mayan calendar," says Moises.

"I believe in astrology! And in the influence of the planets on us humans, too," declares a young American woman. – "Do you see the Pleiades up there? Those tiny stars in a single cluster?" She points and explains to her female friend, who appears, however, to have her doubts about both stars and people.

"I shall show you," insists the first speaker, and before we know where we are she has flung off her clothes and cries:

"My hands and feet are stars and my head is a star. Now I lie in the same direction as the constellation – now!" and suddenly the "Rattle of the Rattlesnake," called tzab by the Mayan astronomers, has fallen down at our astonished feet on the temple stairway. Thus our American is transformed into a fireworks of celestial bodies arranging themselves in well-known constellations, one after the other.

"The Great Bear!" she announces. "But with too short a tail, that you must imagine projected from my right hand. And if you bind my star-feet and prolong the line you come to the polestar."

"The polestar was one of the Mayan gods and the protector of travellers. He was married to the young Moon goddess. The Maya had many both subterranean and celestial gods, just hear: The Fat god, the Black god called Ek Chuak, the god 'The Lizard's House' with his spouse, the Rainbow lady, the Bat god, the Bee god…"

Enrique muses without taking his eyes from the Great Bear on the temple stairway. "Come and help me, I haven't enough stars for 'the Virgin,'" cries our naked teacher in stellar interpretation; but before some willing pupil has had time to volunteer the moon disappears behind a ragged cloud. The lords on the stucco frescos withdraw into the darkness. The performance is at an end and the stars guiltily resume their places in the sky. A cold current of air makes me shiver. Strange noises like the murmur of voices and sighs come from the interior of the temple and mingle with the jungle symphony.

"Are there still jaguars in the jungle round here, Moises?"

"Listen, perhaps you will hear it!" says Moises. – "When the jaguar roars all the other animals fall silent. His fearful roar still hovers, as it were, in the darkness for a long, long time. And his roaring is heard over great distances. Even to Sweden!"

"To Sweden?"

"Yes, even to Sweden," he repeats. He is silent; but we all know he is preparing a fresh narrative. After some minutes of pregnant silence to heighten the tension he begins: "Why just there, in your strange country (Marianne Greenwood is Swedish!) at the Pole, where the sun shines uninterruptedly day and night in summer and never peeps over the horizon in winter, did a lady suddenly hear that a jaguar was calling her to Palenque?"

"The jaguar has a magical significance in all Indian religions. We all know of the mysterious Olmec's jaguar-god with the face of a baby. The jaguar is the nocturnal image of the sun. The sun's shadows, so to speak," says Enrique. "The flying dragon of the Maya has a jaguar's head and his body consists of clouds…"

Moises does not allow himself to be disturbed and goes on: "In any case, this Swedish lady heard how the jaguar was calling her hither urgently, demandingly, and with such persistence that she had no choice but to betake herself headlong to Palenque as if to an assignation with a lover. Just after she arrived she began to wander about in the jungle around these ruins and the river, seeking her jaguar. He called her. She answered. His voice was now quite close. She was sure it was her he was calling and she was completely deaf to our mockery and joking. "One day news came that the spoor of a jaguar had been found near the ruins. I tried to warn our friend against wandering alone without arms, but she only smiled and assured me that she was not afraid. He was her friend. He did not wish her any harm."

Moises falls silent and appears to be listening. Do we not all hear a distant roaring from the forest? We are all agog. But all we can distinguish is a gentle rustling, the purling, lapping sound of the little river, the song of the cicadas and the croaking of frogs.

"So one day the jaguar had been right up to the outskirts of the village. Never in living memory had a jaguar been found so near to an inhabited place. Without informing my Swedish friend, who was still straying about in the forest like an unhappy Ophelia, a party set out on a jaguar hunt. I will not weary you with an account of how such an expedition is planned and carried out. The point is that they succeeded in killing the animal."

"When the Swedish lady returned from the jungle and was walking down the village street she met the cortège with the jaguar, which had already been flayed and was being carried on a pole between two of the hunters. It was the biggest specimen I have ever seen. When she saw the jaguar she uttered a frightful shriek, so heart-rending that I still have it in my ear. She flung herself over the creature's body, embraced it, wept and accused herself loudly for the animal's death. We had at last to tear her away from her dead darling by main force. For three days and three nights we heard her incessant weeping and lamentation, which filled our hearts with grief and pangs of conscience; and then one day she was gone, without leaving a trace. Palenque has never heard more of her. I miss her. She was a real Maya, although she had the misfortune to be born a little far away." Moises falls silent.

The moon takes the opportunity to peep out again and light up the filigree spire on the temple roof of the sun.

There is a Mexico one can see and another Mexico underneath, buried in the earth, yet still palpably alive. The more one digs the higher one seems to get – like falling upwards!

Tulum, the Mayan Acropolis. I live in a house without walls. The floor is the sand of the beach, white with crushed shells. There are no windows or doors and the wind lives with me when it is not playing hide-and-seek on the sea or among Don Felipe's thousand coconut palms. The striped cat streaks among the poles as in a giant skeleton. Just as the Indian does not stop living because he dies, but only passes over to another existence, so the trees from the surrounding forest go on living when they become "palapa" houses. Bound together with the same lianas as in the forest and not wounded by a single nail, stakes and poles retain their original form. The same orchids and creepers cling around them, and in the palm roof, so thick that not a drop of the heaviest tropical rainfall can penetrate it, live the same crabs, lizards and insects as in the forest from which it was originally taken, without being in the slightest disturbed by the people it now shelters. The blue of the sea fills space and thought alike. My private life is like washing hung out to dry, but this is compensated by the reciprocal view into our neighbours' dwellings. Don Felipe's hut is located a little deeper in the palm groves, and as I swing lazily in my Yucatán hammock I can see right into the shack of my nearest neighbour, André the fisherman. Hope he comes home with fish from the sea – or maybe lobster, of which succulent beasts there is an abundance among the coral reefs.

The naked Maya dog comes wagging his tail. The sunlight shimmers on his smooth violet skin, which does not boast a single hair. He is as slenderly built as the greyhounds on an old French tapestry, in contrast to his ancestors on Mayan frescoes and clay pots. In ancient times these hairless dogs were fattened and esteemed a culinary treat, as tasty as tepescuinte meat, a paca species.

Not that Don Felipe would be capable of killing an animal. Nor does this gentle and noble descendant of the Maya eat any animal that gives birth to living young – which was only the other day what saved the shark from being flung into Doña Dimitria's cauldron. All the members of the family are Seventh-day Adventists, and on Saturdays all the neighbours come to Don Felipe's and sing psalms with a gusto that even drowns the otherwise eternal sound of the sea. Doña Dimitria's voice is then heard above those of all the others in a high soprano, and all the starry-eyed lads sing in unison at the tops of their voices.

Since Don Felipe has read the Gospel about the Maya's new god he is unwilling to answer all my questions concerning Tulum's temple ruins, to be seen a little further north on the coast. Who was the "Falling god" (Dios Descendente), he who on all the frescos above the entrances to the temples is seen rushing precipitously down through the ether with terrifying velocity like a "sky-diver" who has left his parachute at home? Did this Mayan Icarus in his feathered garb represent the setting sun, or was he the Bee-god in what was called "The land of roe-deer and honey?" When I think of the matter it strikes me that I saw more beehives than human dwellings along the white highway through the jungle and the cactus thickets of Quintana Roo.

Is it out of courtesy to this god that all temple buildings have the unusual form of truncated pyramids with the base uppermost? Was it so that from the god's celestial vantage point Tulum should appear mightier? But the portals, on the other hand, are broader at the bottom than at the top, so he can enter there with his feet on the ground after landing safely. Or is the explanation perhaps that the outward-leaning walls give a better perspective and at the same time enhance the play of light and shade on stucco frescoes and other decorations? Alas! the thick wall that on three sides helps the sea to encircle Tulum has been able to keep out neither the pirates of a former age nor the modern vandal, and all the beautiful frescoes and murals can only be divined as pale ghosts from bygone times.

Nowhere but in Greece have I had such a feeling of Greece as in Tulum, today's Tulún on the north-east coast of Yucatán. The light, the colors, or rather the lack of colors, the whole atmosphere, the people, the sun-bleached bare landscape. To sit on a stone bench in one of the intimate little "adoratorios" open to all four points of the compass and contemplate the surrounding country and its history is a great spiritual experience.

El Castillo, which stands on an 18-meter-high limestone rock facing the sea, as blue as the sacred color of the Maya, looks like a mirage or a memory of the Acropolis, while all the mythology of the Mediterranean begins to blend in one's mind with Mayan legends an myths. Among broken pillars and ruined stairways live giant lizards and iguanas; as unmoving as the flying dragons on the frescoes, they belong more to fairy-tale than to reality. The snake basks under his befeathered compeer, that writhes like an arabesque among flowers and corn-cobs around dancing high priests and Maya lords, while the hiero-glyphs slowly disappear into ever completer illegibility with their secrets.

This was the town which the members of the first Spanish expedition under the command of Grijalva saw when they passed with their four ships along the coast of Yucatán in the year 1518, and which their chronicler Juan Diaz thus describes: "… so big that we do not consider the town of Seville to be bigger and better … with a very high tower…" Tulum was then known as Zamá. Even at that time one of the two Spaniards who were shipwrecked on the way to Cuba from Darien and were bought as slaves by Kinich, the lord of Zamá, lived here. When, some years later, Cortes arrived in Cozumel, one of these slaves, Gerónimo de Aguilar, joined the conquistadors, while his friend refused to abandon his Maya, saying: "Brother Aguilar, I am married and have three children, and the

Indians have made me burgo-master and made me a captain in their army in war-time. Go thou, and God be with thee, but as for me, with my face tattooed and with pierced lobes for ear-plugs, what would the Spaniards say if they saw me in this guise? And look at my beautiful children and lovely wife … and so forth."

This Spaniard converted to Maya, Gonzalo Guerrero, was afterwards made a lord and led the Maya in their defence against the Spaniards at Chetumal, until he was killed in Honduras in the year 1536.

Not only brother Guerrero had the lobes of his ears pierced in Yucatán!

I remember how my stately neighbour Higinia in the fishing village of Sisal insisted on the vital importance of having holes in one's ears, and that I could not be regarded as fully developed without these. "One has earrings to shut out evil spirits and to protect the soul, so it does not slip out of one," said Higinia severely. – "At the full moon we shall have a proper feast and I will make the finest holes you have ever seen."

I tried to object that in the time of the Maya it was the man who had holes not only in his ears but also in his nose, to be able to place an ornament there on feast-days. The holes in the ears were to be so big that a turkey's egg could pass through them. However, my objections were of no avail, and, as the phases of the moon advanced, feverish preparations were made for the feast, which would be a welcome opportunity to break the grey monotony of the workaday world. The girls curled their long, lank Indian hair in a thousand locks, huipiles and lace-edged petticoats were ironed, and the gold earrings that had been left as a pledge with the grocer were reclaimed with the promise that on the morning after the feast they should be back in their places in the tradesman's shoe-box under the counter. Don Valiche was specially invited with his gramophone with horn, an important item to ensure the success of the feast. Doña Rosa baked thousands of tortillas and the turkey bade an eternal farewell to the yellow flowers in the back garden to take part in the feast in the form of a filling for tacos, a sort of tortilla sandwich. All the fish the men managed to draw out of the sea were immediately transformed into tequila for the thirsty throats of the village. And at last the full moon appeared, as of course it always does. Nowhere can a feast have the intensity it has in Mexico. I danced jarana and boleros with my fisher friends and forgot all about the occasion for all this excitement. But when at everybody's request Don Pedrín had sung of faith, hope, and love with his caressing aguardiente voice the serious moment arrived when I was to have my ears pierced. The dancing ceased. At a sign from Doña Higinia our Mayan troubadour stopped in the middle of a stanza. Everyone took a generous gulp of tequila to strengthen his nerves. I took two to give myself courage. A chair was placed like a guillotine in the middle of the floor under a solitary electric bulb. In absolute and dramatic silence I was led forth like a sacrificial lamb to the altar. Everyone crowded round, and I must confess that I did feel a trifle nervous. A thought crossed my somewhat befuddled mind: "How many tequilas had Higinia already drunk?" But all too late. Advancing as slowly as a high priestess Higinia approached, clad in her wide embroidered huipil with the bordeaux-colored shawl draped gracefully about her. In her hand she held a

horrendous darning needle
of the kind that is used to sew
sails for the fishing boats. She
took a firm grip of my ear and
thrust the needle resolutely
through the lobe. Not so bad.
A collective sigh rose from the
spectators. Now for the next!
It seemed to me that she was
taking rather a long time
about it, but finally she
announced triumphantly:
"Ready!" – A mirror was
brought and I was able to
admire my new decorations:
a thread was threaded through
each hole and tied in a fine
rosette. One thread was red
and the other green, just as
on the Mexican flag!
The one hole was a fine little
one, while the other was so
big that I could very easily
imagine a turkey's egg
passing through it! Whether
they turned out thus on
account of linguistic misunder-
standing or as the result of
copious glasses of tequila
I cannot say to this day.
I wonder if the feast for
brother Gonzalo was some-
thing in the same style though
with more feathers and pomp,
perhaps. Or as a little
sacrifice to his new gods?
But since it has become old-
fashioned to throw beautiful
Mayan maidens in the sacred
cenotes – natural grottos –
for the gratification of the
rain-god, and there was as

yet no cinema in our little
village, we had to content
ourselves with what entertainment was to be had.
I have struggled up from the
hammock. André has made
me a present of a magnificent
lobster that is being boiled
over the open fire behind Don
Felipe's house while we sit
chatting on the terrace.
The palms are swaying in the
evening breeze and the
turquoise blue of the sea
darkens to inky black.
Doña Dimitria reminds one
forcibly of Jaina's corpulent
clay ladies, who have a full-
grown, sometimes bearded
man like a child in their lap.
She may also be a
descendant of the goddess of
fertility or Ixchel the mother-
goddess, who was
worshipped especially on
Cozumel, the island opposite
where we live. It was from
there that Don Felipe once
fetched his bride when he
came sailing with coconuts
in his little bark. Dimitria has
given him many sloe-eyed
Maya babies, and not a year
passes without an addition to
the family. For every new
arrival Felipe digs some deep
holes in the sand and plants
more coconut palms, and
further to bolster the economy
he sells nuts and soft drinks
to thirsty tourists whom he
allows to pitch their tents

under the palms at the lagoon. As thanks for this hospitality they leave behind them all the rubbish the town has. Doña Dimitria makes more and more tortillas for the growing family, both her own and those of the tourists.

"There's room for all of us," says Don Felipe. – "We are all sisters and brothers."

His amiable face shines, but suddenly he looks sad. – "But who will buy my rancho? Why should I now sell my home? As far as that goes I have no papers to prove my ownership, though I got the land from the government 40 years ago. The lawyer in Merida is asking many thousand pesos to get me the papers – more pesos than there are coconuts along the whole coast, I should think."

It is true that Don Felipe is the only one of the original Maya here who has a rancho at the seaside. The land at the coast to the north and to the south has been bought up by banking families from the capital or by American fishing clubs, and nowhere but at my host's place may one even bathe from the lovely sandy beaches bordered with coconut palms. These twentieth-century conquistadors have even been able to forbid the native fishermen to cast a single hook or net in the river where the sweet waters of the lagoon empty into the sea as they have done for thousands of years. Everything is reserved for the few but wealthy tourists who come here by air. But what is Mexico's biggest industry if not the "peaceful" conquest of our age, tourism?

I fear that Don Felipe will soon be requested to retire further inland with his family to tame the forest to a new "palapa" and the swamp to produce coconut palms.

As we have only a few places being blessed with electricity, radio and TV have not yet killed conversation. Don Felipe is a good narrator and tells us many tales. He speaks of the mysterious little temples which one finds scattered about the Yucatán peninsula, and which according to popular belief are still used by a dwarf people hidden in the darkness of the forests; he tells of the puma on the beach and of the many strange statues and pots he found in the earth far beyond marshes and savannahs when in his youth he cleared virgin ground for plantations of palms. "Nothing came of it. I was too young then," says Felipe. To this day no one else has strayed to that part, he assures us, for it is inhumanly difficult only to find the place. One must first pass through a real labyrinth of streams, lagoons and water-logged bogs in a canoe; and one must then continue on foot through endless brushwood where one may easily get lost, and where the thorns of the bushes jealously protect all treasures sunk for many centuries in a slumber like that of the Sleeping Beauty.

The flickering of the paraffin lamp is now all that separates us from a deep blue darkness, and the palms have disappeared into the night, leaving a gentle rustling mingled with the song of the sea behind them. The creaking of the hammock is almost compact, and Doña Dimitria's flute-like voice is heard calling the children drinking in every syllable of daddy's narration. "Cox wenel men le Ka-no tu quetch!" she cries in Maya, which means: "Come, let us go and sleep, the hammock is weeping for you!"

In Mexico one must live among the people, laugh and suffer together with them if one is to feel the real extent of their nobility and beauty. To pass the frontier separating the poor from the rest of the population in a strange country and to be accepted by them is almost as impossible as it is simple to be admitted to the world of the wealthy. Once, however, I succeeded in becoming completely – body and soul – a member of Mexico's "pueblo," though this was involuntary and it nearly cost me my life to attain to this experience. At the same time I spent the three most beautiful weeks of a life that has known very many vicissitudes.

A little bell rang. The sound lingered on for an eternity before I recovered consciousness. But where was I? Light began to filter through the half-closed lids of my eyes. A heavenly music streamed over me and cradled me as if in clouds. I was dead, I was in heaven – it came to me suddenly. Organ music and bright voices in jubilant unison, what could they be but angels? I tried to close my eyes tight to delay the moment of complete awakening and knowing. But my curiosity was too much for me, as it always is. I peered towards the light but saw only a haze in which shadows slowly floated past. As if on a blurred copy of an Eisenstein film of the Mexican revolution one could dimly make out white-clad farm labourers with enormous straw sombreros and triangles – perhaps women clad in black? – motionless and moving, the latter striding slowly over the field of vision and balancing something square on their heads. Beings like veiled angels mingled with the crowd. Ah-ha! So it was true! One flew straight up in the air when one died and found oneself in the paradise that is located just above the place where one has breathed one's last. I was in the Mexican heaven! More precisely, in the sublimated Mexico just above Guadalajara. And the angels who were singing were "tapatío"-angels! Without mariachis!

I was dead, so much was certain! But the shadow of a doubt was left in my mind. Where did this terrible cold come from? What was the point of my running away from the ice-cold Ultima Thule of my forbears if Mexico's paradise was no warmer? Was it perhaps the coldness of the grave? Something, I thought confusedly, did not add up. But before I had time to decide on some other alternative I heard a commanding voice:

"Abre tus ojos divinos!"
"Open your divine eyes!"
In Spanish! The angels spoke Spanish! And my eyes were heavenly! No more doubt. I was dead. Proof positive! So I might as well look around in my new world. The picture was less blurred and I could

now see an endless double row of beds disappearing towards the horizon. The shadows took form, but continued to look like Mexican farm-hands in white garments and women clad in shawls, balancing something square on their heads. The veiled beings slipped past like figures in a dream.

"Tacos! Enchiladas!" a voice was calling. Ah-ha! so people ate tacos also in the Mexican heaven! I turned my head. At my bedside sat a fellow I had never seen before. When he saw me he smiled. He was as beautiful as an angel.

A little bell rang. The sound lingered on in the morning light and again it seemed an eternity before I regained consciousness. I was shaking with cold. I was alive. Memories returned like a film run backwards. Had I not confessed my sins? No, the padre who had been hastily summoned had refused me confession. In my mind's eye I could still see him disappearing down the corridor between the innumerable beds, running so fast that his caftan flapped about his legs. Protestant! Worse than if I had said anything else beginning with "pro!" For that matter, he had no time to listen to the sins of a whole life that had, as it were, been stacked in one great heap and must perforce be gabbled in a single last breath.

Other memories returned. That on Friday evening I had been carried, half dead from loss of blood, to the Cruz Roja, Guadalajara's "civilian" hospital, regarded as the hospital of the poor and death's waiting room, for an urgent operation. That my whole fortune amounted to three pesos and that I knew no one in the whole town, apart from a Mexican youth I had tried to help out of prison. It was Sunday morning. The nuns' Mass in the chapel next door was over. The march of the pot-bearers continued as before. For it was chamber-pots they were balancing on their heads. The unmoving triangles were really women; waiting and watching over sick relatives, they crouched on the floor at the respective bedsides day and night.

At my bedside sat a beautiful ranchera, Soledad. There she had sat for two whole nights to see that I did not hurt myself on the needles and that I got blood and serum into my veins in due order. The blood, of a very uncommon sort, had been donated by a Mexican woman named María de los Ángeles Cervantes, which augured well for continued writings, I was pleased to imagine.

The white-clad men were relatives of the sick who had come to visit the latter. When little by little I had eaten some of the food provided by the hospital, served in tin mugs with neither spoon nor fork but with tortillas, I understood that it was not suitable even for very healthy and resistant stomachs. However, vendors of tacos trotted up and down between the 86 beds in the enormous corridor that was our ward, much as their counterparts in Europe do on a railway platform before the departure of a train. But the fellow at my bedside? In due course I got the explanation of his existence. He had been admitted to the department for mental cases, but as he was considered harmless he was allowed to move around freely. When I was taken to the operating theatre this Gerardo was struck by a glance from my heavenly blue eyes, and since then he had sat faithfully beside my bed in hopes of catching another beam.

For that matter he saved my life – together with the doctors and sisters, of course – by bringing me every day a large glass of choco-milk with a raw egg beaten into it.

When my neighbours also discovered that I never ate, they began generously sharing with me their fruit and tacos, chicken and other good things from their baskets. This soon brought my strength back, naturally together with the excellent treatment I got from my doctors: my skilful surgeon, my "swordsman" ("Espadachín") Guillermo Esqueda, a gentleman with exuberant mustachios, burning black eyes and a great fund of charm and humour; the resident doctor, as handsome as Maupassant's Bel Ami; and Irma Vargas, the young medical student who had assisted at the operation, and who used to come and cheer me up with poems of her own and inspiring friendship.

The chaos of the outer world did not penetrate to this absolute order, this ant-heap of poverty which had its own laws. Here, what was unimportant disappeared, the accent was on essentials. The feeling of human commonalty was greater than in any other collective, I am sure; and the understanding between the patients was complete. Those who had been operated upon were looked after by those who had not yet had their operation. One surrendered oneself with complete confidence to the solicitude and care of one's sisters-in-need; with a feeling of absolute security one lived in a world where moans and groans were shared by all and laughter was the only cheap entertainment. So we laughed at all the rats that ran relay races under the beds when the electric bulbs had been screwed out for the night so they should not be stolen; at the awkwardness and inconvenience at the WC's – a description of these would shake any socialized community to its foundations. And we laughed at the patients who after their operation took their first tottering steps supported by two fellow-patients; at Elvira's floor-cloth, as grey as the melancholy of the outside world, when she dried the floor; at the stories of life on a ranch at Chapala narrated by Doña Rita, the grand old Indian always wrapped in her dark blue shawl; we laughed at married men, presidents and kings; at the scramble for power and money in the world outside, and a great deal else besides.

One day my swordsman said brusquely, though his eyes were smiling: "You know, Mariana, it's about time you went home. You make my patients laugh so that their only half closed wounds burst open!

There I stood on the hospital steps. The sun was shining as it always does in Guadalajara. I still had my three pesos in my hand. But I was very rich. I had as many new friends as beds in the ward, I was one of them.

Life is a good stage manager. It was Irma, now a doctor at Seguro Social, who at the last moment saved the life of a French friend of mine after a bad accident in Puerto Vallarta quite recently. And sometimes I ride on Doña Rita's horses on her rancho in Santa Cruz on the shores of Lake Chapala, and then, over dried shrimps and beer, we laugh again at our many memories and know that our lives are parallel and inseparable for ever. We get sisters and brothers on our way through life.

The frontiers between Mexico and the outside world are like rivers without bridges. As soon as we have passed the frontier we find ourselves in a totally different world, where nothing is like anything we have ever seen before. The same word suddenly means something quite different and is incomprehensible to us. Such simple words as yes and no are here a completely different language, that one has to learn, a philosophy like "mañana," which does not just mean tomorrow, later, perhaps never, but represents a whole style of life. Silence is a language. Lies are often a form of politeness or ordinary tact, the special virtue of the simple people. Even time is different, and it is impossible to set one's clock by Mexican time, for here eternity has been built into the clockwork of all timepieces.

Señor Malacara and the shark-hunt:

I am swimming in the sea together with a turtle a good deal bigger than myself. The sun blazes down from the zenith — we are precisely on the Tropic of Cancer and it is noon. The little cove where we are swimming is sheltered by large rock formations and these, Señor Malacara has assured me, keep out the sharks. Where the fine white sandy beach vanishes into the shade of a grove of tall coconut palms I see a figure on a donkey emerging from the shadows. The figure dismounts and tethers the donkey to a palm and, machete in mouth, starts climbing a palm at a suitable distance from his Rosinante. So this is where Señor Malacara gets the coconuts he brings to my hut at sunset! Presently I hear the sound of dislodged pebbles and a rustling – and there he comes on his donkey up the almost imperceptible path, so steep that for a moment I see only his wide sombrero and the ears of his donkey.

He lays the nuts, which he has opened, together with some yellow-ripe mangoes and perhaps a couple of fresh eggs on the invisible threshold, then, if he sees that I am writing, he withdraws discreetly. Señor Malacara has a great respect for those who can read and write; he is, moreover, intuitive and a perfect gentleman. Perhaps, too, he wants to avoid once more having to answer my eternal question as to when the shark-hunters are coming. "Wait only a little longer, Señora, por favor! Mañana!"

Señor Malacara, Mr. "Ugly Face," looks just as if Picasso had painted him. One seems to see him in profile and full face at one and the same time, however he turns his head. His nose is flattened and seems pushed to one side. One of his slanting eyes squints so outrageously that the pupil seems almost to touch the bridge of his nose, while the other eye sweeps the horizon, so that it is almost impossible to escape his field of vision. The one cheek is puffed out, while the other is caved in under a high cheek-bone, indicating his Indian descent. This is also evident in his jet-black hair and dark complexion.

Like all good human beings, however, Señor Malacara becomes more beautiful the longer one knows him, and, far from inspiring loathing on account of his ugliness, he is evidently Chamela's Robin Goodfellow and soul.

Children, who far more often than not have a sounder understanding of real values than their – as they used to be called – elders and betters, cluster around him, are allowed to ride his donkey, listen to his tales. "Tell us, Señor Malacara, por favor, tell us about the octopus that was so hungry that he ate up his own arms!" – "Tell us about the pirates that built Castillo de Aragón and about the treasure . . ."

True enough, just below my hut are the remains of the old French pirate castle – ruined walls hidden among bushes and leaves, rounded corner turrets. The whole of Chamela's wide semicircular bay in which nestle the seven mountainous islands must have been an ideal retreat for pirates in the old days.

And it was Señor Malacara who gave me this little house,

without which I might still have been wandering over Jalisco's grey and wild mountains without ever discovering this paradise. And how was it I came at all to this sequestered bay? Well, I am out shark-hunting! I have heard that somewhere on Mexico's Pacific coast sharks are hunted from horseback with harpoons. The procedure is as follows: the hunter-fishermen throw quantities of bloody meat as bait into the shark-infested waters. Sharks are commonest where fresh water flows out into the sea to form lagoons and shallows. When the sharks, excited by the bait, come in schools, the horsemen ride out into the sea, hurl their harpoons, then face about and gallop up on the beach. The harpoon is fastened to a long rope which is firmly lashed to the pommel of the saddle. In this way the shark is dragged ashore and despatched with machetes. This strikes me as a sport for the courageous, and I have long had an unsettled account with the sharks in the Pacific.

Are there now any shark-hunters on horseback in Chamela as I heard it rumoured? Alas! the only mounted man I have seen here is Señor Malacara on his Rosinante. But he has promised me shark-hunting and it would be an insult to his dignity to doubt his word – therefore I wait patiently.

I see, by the way, that he has now left the palm grove on his donkey, and I crawl up to sun myself in the shallows where the sea-swell washes up shells with every breath. So I spend my days idling and bathing, and sometimes my typewriter catches a few words on their flight with the wind through my little house without walls. I ask Señor Malacara about the shark-hunt every day now. It has become a standing joke with us. Perhaps he sometimes looks a little worried when I say that I must continue my quest for the shark-hunters. Every day black clouds gather over the La Purificación Mountains, whose highest peak is over 9,000 feet above sea-level. Everyone is waiting for the first rains – and when they do come we shall be isolated from the rest of the world by rivers in flood and without bridges.

One night, after falling to sleep in my hammock, I am woken up by a terrible hullabaloo. A terrific wind is sweeping the mountain-side, rushing through the hut and making the sea growl menacingly. The hammock is swinging jerkily as a flash of lightning illuminates the hut for a split second, only to leave it in intenser darkness. I try to sleep, but in vain. The thunder reverberates in the distance and the clamour of the sea is everywhere. By the time the storm has abated, a twilight – the twilight preceding the dawn – is stealing into the air. So I get up, dress in the semi-darkness and go out, following the path in the direction of the stream's disemboguing into the bay. For the first time I behold Nature's awakening in Chamela! From the emerald meadows of the lagoon a light mist is rising, revealing white herons among lilac water-hyacinths. The first light comes hesitatingly. Then, almost without transition, triumphant day is chasing away all the doubt and the terrors of the night. Dawn and dusk come suddenly in the tropics, like an assault. Suffused with happiness I wander through the forest down to the delta-land of the widening stream. At the edge of the forest I stop dead in my tracks. There, out in the shallow water Señor Malacara is galloping about on his grey donkey. A long rope is lashed to the pommel of his saddle. He swings the harpoon over his head and its shining steel point catches a sunbeam as he hurls it into the sea. He wheels the donkey abruptly shoreward, spurs the poor beast with non-existent spurs and utters a loud cry as the little donkey gallops up the beach amid flying spray. The harpoon is plunged in a dog . . . Malacara jumps off the donkey and rushes with uplifted machete at his prize, pretending to stab it again and again. I know that the poor dog's carcase has already been lying on the beach for many days. Malacara flings the dog into the sea again, sets off at a gallop on his donkey and repeats the whole perfor-mance – the dog is both bait and prize, Malacara all the shark-hunters in Chamela in one person and his donkey all their fiery steeds!

I am standing in the shadow of the trees. So absorbed is he in his little game that Señor Malacara has not seen me. He knows that I never come this way so early in the morning. I turn round and withdraw cautiously into the forest – the trees will keep my silence and my secret.

Then there are Mexicans, remains of the original inhabi-tants, who speak their own language, have their own morals, religions and cultures:

the Indians in the high Sierra Madre and in Chiapas' deep forests. I once visited the Huichole Indians of Nayarit. I was accompanied by a youth of Huichole extraction who could speak their language and was supposed to protect me. His name was Pedro, a fat timid boy of 19 who earned a livelihood by copying the patterns on the Huichole "nearikas" for the "Casa de Artesanía" in Guadalajara. These are embroidered creations in wool on board, full of symbols and signs interwoven with abstract representations of animals and plants and originally inspired by dreams caused by the hallucinogenic drug peyote, as the Huicholes are fervent devotees of the cult. To get this spineless cactus their shamans make a pilgrimage of 300 miles every year to their sacred land Wirikuta in the San Luis Potosí desert. "El Macho 75," or the Huichole Volkswagen. We reached the airport before the frost had left the deserted streets of Tepic and the morning star had paled in the sky. We were soon seated in a one-engine plane which looked and sounded like a sewing machine and was only slightly bigger than one, and soaring almost

vertically towards the tremendously high Sierra Madre Occidental. We seemed to flap our wings like a bird to get over the peak, and I had a feeling that if it hadn't been for the draught we should never have made it. After being flung about in space for some time we prepared to land on a strip consisting of a slope with an inclination of about 45 degrees and ending at the brink of a precipice. However, we landed safely in Guadalupe Ocotlán, a little village looking for all the world like a handful of toys scattered at the bottom of a huge valley. We started at once to enquire for some suitable locomotion for the continuation of our trip. At Don Francisco's rancho we found what we were looking for. Don Francisco, with more smiles than teeth in his mouth and a sparse beard to indicate his Latin ancestry, declared himself ready to accompany us and put his black mule, answering to the futuristic name "El Macho 75," at our disposition. "El Macho 75," together with another mule borrowed from a neighbour, made two mules for three people, which was considered a fair deal – not for the mules of course, but

who asks their opinion?
After a night of freezing like dogs on raffia mats we had some tortillas and fresh water and mounted the mules – I on the "Macho 75" and Francisco on the other mule while Pedro walked behind. The path was so steep that I had all my work cut out just to remain on the back of my mount. This wonderful animal, that I baptized "The Huichole Volkswagen," to the great glee of my companions, seemed to be able to walk on nothing and carry everything. Sometimes the trail slanted downwards so terrifyingly that he seemed to disappear in front of me, ears and all, while I saw on all sides nothing but precipices, till I almost believed him to be a sort of winged and fabulous creature from Greek mythology and that we had taken off into space together. Sometimes he seemed to be climbing straight up into the sky and I had to hang round his neck for dear life, not to slide back into the thousands of feet below. But he planted his feet between the sharp loose stones with absolute assurance and showed not a trace of nervousness.
The silence was enormous, and the solitude only measurable in terms of the distance from civilization.

Up and down the mountains appearing endlessly before us we rode all day long. Save for a few birds and lizards we saw not a single being, and there was not a sign of any human dwellings. When night fell I felt as though I had been sitting on "El Macho" all my life, and that we had become a strange sort of mountain-centaur, inseparable for life. The moon rolled up over the mountains and took over the lighting job. Strange shadows followed us and in the vast silence I fancied I could hear the stars. Occasionally the silence would be briefly broken by the wings of unseen birds or some rolling stones hitting the bottom of the precipice. Suddenly my mule reared up on his hind legs and uttered a horrid ass-cry into the night. Swaying slowly with the breeze as if suspended by a rope from the branch of a tree, there was a skin-and-bone dried-to-yellow coyote with his mouth open in a soundless bowling to the moon.
Finally, when having given up all hope of arriving anywhere that night, we saw a fire in the distance. The mules quickened their trot and we soon found ourselves at El Rancho de la Laguna Seca, the goal set for

the day. After some tortillas with salt and chile pepper and a glass of water I fell on a dried and untanned cow-skin in an empty hut lit by a piece of Ocote wood stuck in a crack in the adobe wall. How hard that cow must have been in life to leave such a hard skin for posterity! And how cold it was! Sierra Madre, wasn't it cold! I was happy when I heard people and animals wake up and I rushed out for breakfast – tortillas with salt and chile pepper and fresh spring water.

After breakfast the women immediately sat down to embroider and make conversation, both a great art with the Huicholes. We seemed to be sitting on the roof of the world – as far as the eye could reach one saw only wilderness, mountains. A Huisache tree was shedding its yellow blossoms over me as I sat watching the children play with the silvery grey feathers of a dove they were plucking. They threw the feathers high in the air and ran after them with excited screams, and if it had not been for the stone wall between us and nothing they would have sprung into the sky like small Icaruses in search of the sun.

Señor Maximilian, our host, was leaving with his family to visit the rancho of his nearest neighbour, where a fiesta was to be held and a bull sacrificed – why didn't we come along instead of continuing east? Certainly – a fiesta is a fiesta and more important than anything! Don Francisco returned to Ocotlán on his neighbour's mule but left us "El Macho 75," making one mule for two people.

The walk to the nearest neighbour turned out to be a whole day's uninterrupted struggle over the same impossible mountains. Not until late afternoon did El Rancho de los Mangos appear, a lush oasis in the grey landscape. As we entered the plaza we were greeted by the host of the fiesta. Before his hut was an altar adorned with many "god-eyes" symbolizing prayers for good health, gourd votive bowls with different contents, candles, flowers and young corn – all offerings to various gods: "Our Grandpa Fire," "Our Mother Dove Girl," "Grand-father Deer Tail," "Goddess of the Eastern Clouds," etc. The plaza was decorated with gaudy paper garlands, and a huge earthen vessel full of corn for the Huichole aguardiente tesgüino was cooking over an open fire. People were arriving from all directions, many of them dressed in the hand-embroidered Huichole costume.

Suddenly there was a stir – the shaman and his family had arrived. The host turned quickly to receive the feared witch-doctor and invite him to enter his house. From that moment this privilege was refused me, as the shaman officially declared that my presence had a bad influence on his witchcraft.

This shaman had the blackest and most burning eyes I have ever seen, and jet-black hair hanging down under his straw hat. The hat was indeed a masterpiece, so full of ribbons, tassels and feathers that it made me think of a poultry yard at Christmas time. His blouse and pants were so richly embroidered that there was not room for another cross-stitch. I was reminded of the embroidered table-cloth made by my grandma in Sweden. He was also decorated with so many beads, embroidered bags, tassels and pearls that he looked like a dream of a gift-shop.

Next morning we were all up before dawn and sitting round the fire eating fresh tortillas – the best so far – with salt and chile pepper and fresh delicious water to drink. How to describe the three days and nights that followed? How could so few people and animals produce such a fantastic noise in such a big silence? The explosions of home-made rockets; the chanting and the drums; the monotonous squeaking of the fiddles; the stamping of the men dancing; the screaming of drunken men and women; the giggling; the cries of the donkeys, mules and children; the dogs barking, cocks crowing, hens cackling; the bull's lament and his conversation with his future widows; their bitter complaints, and the piercing shrieks and howlings of the shaman. Especially when I approached. Then he would point at me with his befeathered wand and snarl – in Spanish so that I should understand: "Puta! Perra! Puta!" (whore, bitch whore!). This was the signal to the women to repeat, like a Greek chorus: "Puuuuuuuta! Perrrrrra! Puuuuuuuta!" All this noise naturally mingled with the perpetual tortilla-clapping, as monotonous as the shaman's frequent recitals before the altar, the crackling of the fire and the animated conversation.

On the first day slow and

secret ceremonies were held, of which I naturally did not understand very much. The shaman, who had already tasted the tesgüino, looked at the blond intruder from the north with her witch-box, the camera, swore in different languages and spat energetically, reaching my very feet; then he swung his wand and began a terrible howling, followed by a rocket which exploded straight over our sinful heads. This must have been the signal for the fiesta to begin, for the three musicians immediately began to scrape their small home-made fiddles and guitars to produce a screeching that was not to end till three days later.

The dancing, too, had begun. It was a monotonous and simple dance in which the men, standing in a row in front of the women, stamped in time to the music while the women danced more grace-fully, swinging back and forth, swishing their long wide skirts and holding each other's shawls. Suddenly a group of Norteños arrived, people from the North, galloping on mules and spreading fear and confusion on the plaza. They came with their completely different instruments, singing their "rancheros" and hoping to earn some money at the fiesta. Alas! they found only my Pedro willing to listen — and pay! He had become so degenerated in the big city that he did not appreciate the music of his ancestors any more. He had, however, tasted — and liked — their tesgüino very much, and was already zigzagging around. From then on he was constantly followed by the Norteños, who played and sang wherever he went.

I don't know whether it was this day or the following that those fantastic tortillas were served; they were made from lilac-coloured corn and were the best I ever tasted! But as tortillas were the only food I had on this trip it is hard to be precise . . .

The first day of the fiesta was at an end; it grew dark and fires were lit, throwing strange shadows on the scene. The dancing and the marching in procession, led by the musicians, continued, and the shaman recited and danced, making his hocus-pocus, swinging his wand, howling, rolling on the ground, lying like one dead — whether hallucinated by peyote, their earthly symbol for God, or the tesgüino, I cannot say. When I ventured too near, he hurled all sorts of terrible curses and repeated: "Puta! Perra! Puta!," always assisted by his supporters, the Greek chorus. I tried to sleep a little near a fire in a hut, but the intense cold, the giggling of the women, my friend Pedro coming in drunk as a skunk, with his Norteños in attendance to serenade me, all made it rather impossible, and I was happy when dawn arrived and I was able to strengthen myself with some tortillas and water for the culmination and crown of the fiesta, the sacrifice of the bull. Many ceremonies, dances and marching around the plaza with the musicians preceded the great moment. As I was not allowed to come near I only saw the final rite from a distance: the blade of an enormous knife swung by the shaman, who emitted a blood-curdling howl that mingled with the death-bellow of the bull and the explosion of a rocket, so powerful that I thought it would split the heavens in two. There were no signs of fatigue among the participants on this night either. I finally went to sleep in spite of the cold and the noise, only to be awakened by the witch-doctor himself, wanting to sell me his hat with the hundred feathers for 80 pesos. I bought it, not wanting him to put more evil on me than necessary. And so we woke up to the third day of the fiesta, once more beginning with tortillas and spring water. What happened to the bull's meat I cannot say. On this last day the most amusing dances were performed, some sort of a parody of the sacrifice, with one person acting the part of the bull with his hands to his temples in imitation of horns and chasing everybody – presumably to propitiate the bull's spirit for the slaughter. This was the moment Pedro chose to appear on the scene, zigzagging wildly. The pretended bull rushed at him, and only a little push was needed to make my "protector" fall to the ground. The joy of the spectators was comparable to the jubilation at a real bull-fight when the bull is killed by the first sword thrust. The Norteños gathered around the body and played "The Virgin of Maccarena." Then poor Pedro was dragged from the arena to the accompaniment of loud "Olés" from the public. Seeing that there was nothing more to be had, the Norteños mounted their snorting mules and rode away as spectacularly as they had arrived, leaving Pedro by the river to sleep.

That night everything, at last, was wrapped in blessed

silence. Everybody was so utterly exhausted that they slept like logs. Even the animals were silent. And in the morning the cock's crow seemed a dispirited act of duty rather than the triumphant cock-a-doodle-de-dooooo! of the chanticleer heralding the dawn during the fiesta. Meanwhile we prepared to return to Ocotlán, El Macho and I, as Pedro seemed unable to make any decision for himself. When dragged up from the river he was still so drunk that he could not stand on his feet, much less walk, so he was thrown like a sack of potatoes over El Macho's saddle. Then we set off, I walking behind and led by a small starry-eyed boy in embroidered pants. The people shouted "Olé, Olé!" and seemed very friendly – except for the shaman, who refused to say good-bye. He stared with his black burning eyes, some-what red-rimmed by all the tesgüino he had drunk, faintly swinging his befeathered wand, which looked a little used and tired as well, and whispered: "Puta! Perra! Puta!." The echo from the supporters vanished with the wind over the high Sierra Madre. When I got back to Puerto Vallarta I had a high fever and was running a tempera-ture of 105 degrees for five days. And it was only thanks to the intensive care of one of our local shamans, Doctor Rodríguez, that my life was saved. No modern drugs seemed strong enough to fight the curse of the powerful Huichole medicine-man. Perhaps it was his hat, which I squeezed constantly to my chest or had by my side, that transmitted the force enabling my recovery? Weak and exhausted I finally returned to my former life in this tropical Sodom and Gomorrha, wondering whether they really existed, the beautiful Huicholes in the distant mountains – had it all been true, or was it a dream conjured up by my feverish ramblings?
But there was the hat of the shaman!

Puerto Vallarta, April 5th, 1973
Marianne Greenwood

(I still stand in front of that crystal head gazing at the light and reflexes in the veins. And I still understand nothing. In fact, I understand a little less each year. Mexico is the Mexicans, said Fritz. And there are 50 million of them – all passionate, all worth meeting!)

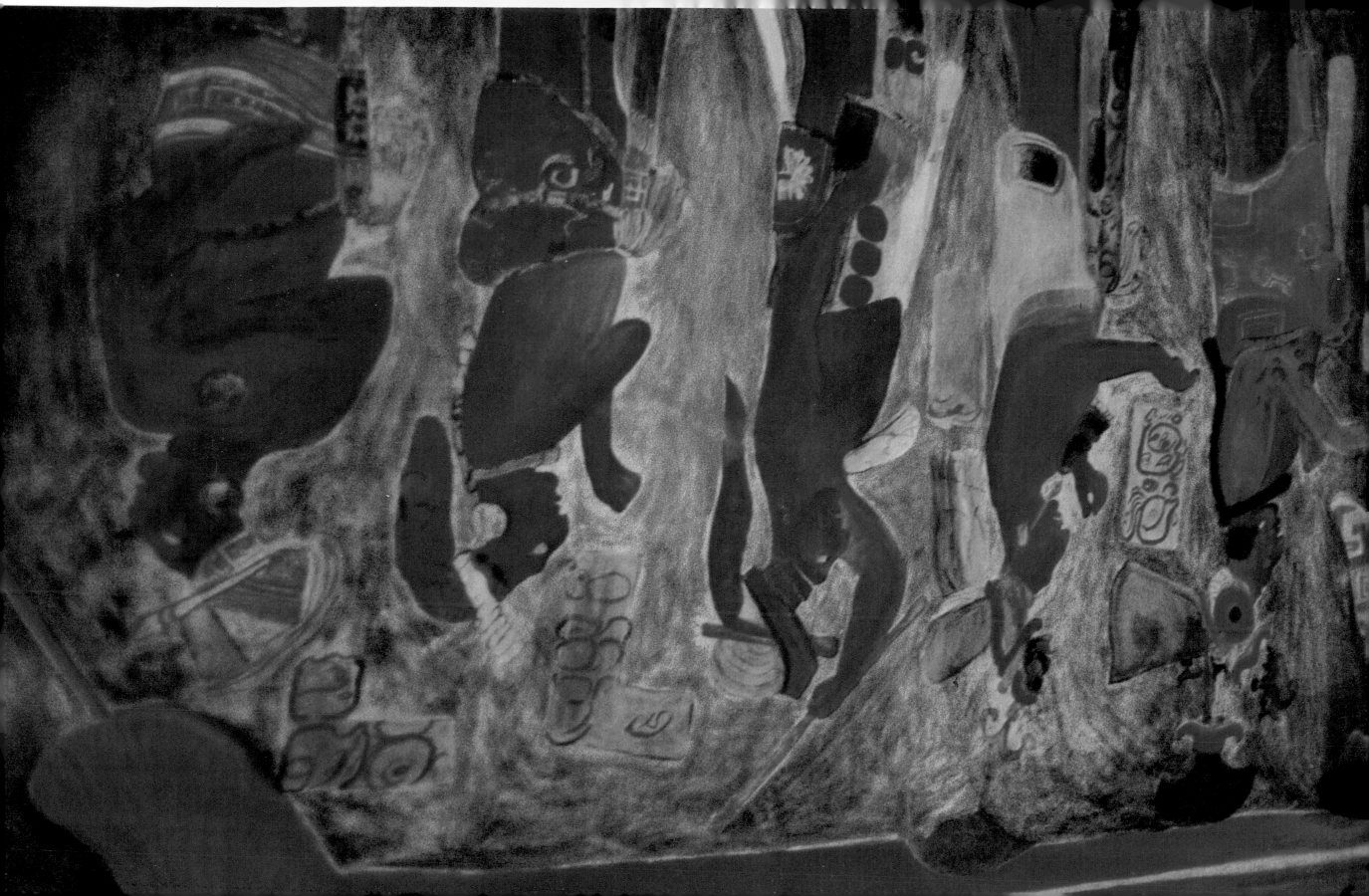

Viva el gran pasado

Explanations of the photos, pages 41 to 52

41 When you study the chronological table, it is quite obvious that the art of the Olmecs and the Maya is not really very old. Even though scientists are rather skeptical when it comes to measurements by the radioactive carbon method on finds in humid tropical areas, there could hardly be any major error involved in the estimated dates. The various civilizations were comprised all within a period ranging from 1500 BC to 1500 AD. The Teotihuacán Civilization (200 BC to 900 AD), the Zapotecan Civilization (400 BC to 1000 AD), the Preclassical Period (500 BC to 300 AD) and the Classical Period (300 AD to 900 AD) of the Maya, and the Aztecan Civilization (1324 to 1521 AD) represent the high points of this epoch. Their architectural and sculptural expressiveness is as fascinating today as ever. The head reproduced in the picture is just one convincing example; like the sculpture on the following double-page, it is preserved

42 in the Anthropological Museum (Museo
43 Nacional de Antropología) in Mexico City. This huge building, inaugurated in 1964, houses relics of all the pre-Spanish civilization periods and boasts of a really exemplary museum concept. The architecture materials and exhibits complement each other in a most harmonious way.

44 In one glass show-case I discovered this group – the size of the 8-in.-high figurines contrasts strongly with the mighty steles and friezes with their embossed surfaces.

45 These pictorial representations are dedicated mainly to religious and cultic scenes. Rite was always at the center of the communal life and experimental ability of the various ancient Mexican cultural manifestations.

46 Many of the representations make you feel that these figures have not yet really become extinct. Way out, in the wide spaces of the country, one can still find many faces so very similar to the figures preserved over the centuries.

47 The very fact that the visitor to the Anthropological Museum can find here a fascinating concentration of old Mexican culture is both a stroke of good luck and an asset to Mexico City's municipal administration. But if time is not your real problem, you will find many excavations beyond the city's limit, such as Teotihuacán, Calixtlahuaca, Tula and Xochicalco, for instance. Xochicalco is the oldest known fortress and one of the highest ranking places of worship. Its location was due to an existing major rise in the ground in a strategically important place. The Toltecan, who continued to defend this stronghold even after their capital Tula had been destroyed by the Chichimecan about 1200 AD, may be considered its founders. Owing to its remarkably well-preserved low reliefs, the 69 ft. x 61 ft. stepsided pyramid plays a major part in the history of old Mexican civilization. The picture shows a detail of the bottom platform relief representing a priest wearing a high-towered plume and jade ornaments on the neck and ears.

48 Bonampak, a place famous for the mural
49 paintings which were only discovered
in 1946, lies in a tropical, humid virgin
forest area north-west of Chiapas. This is
the region where the Lacandones, the last
remnants of the Maya, have been hiding
for centuries, ever since the Spanish
invasion. The Lacandones alone knew of
the unique constructions and paintings.
The frescoes reproduce scenes of feasts,
raids and sacrifices. There is no perspective
at all. Furthermore, all faces are shown in
profile, even when the body appears
frontally.

50 Back in Xochicalco. A look beyond the
51 right-hand outermost corner of the pyramid
base at the strongly clouded Mexican sky.
The about 9-ft.-high lower base is covered
with rock plates into which 2 3/4 to 3 1/2 in.
deep frieze-like reliefs have been carved.
The dominant motif is the representation
of a feathered snake with undulating motions.
All the representations indicate a clear
relationship to the Maya civilization.
There is little doubt that the culture of the
original inhabitants of the place must have
been influenced by the Yucatán people.
This is revealed also by the ball playground which was unearthed in 1935
and which is structurally very similar to the
the ball playgrounds of the northern
highland civilizations. The playground
represented the cosmos, and the ball,
which had to be shot through the hole of
a stone ring without using either the hands
or legs, just by skillful motions of the body,
and particularly of the hips, signified the
movement of the stars.

52 Chichén Itzá, Pyramid of the Kukulcán
Temple. The Toltecs, also called "Itzá,"
conquered the Maya Kingdom in
Yucatán, which had been weakened by
internal conflicts, around 1000 AD. They
brought with them both their highland
architecture and their gods. To honor their
god Kukulcán, they erected a nine-step

pyramid on the square in front of the
warriors' temple. Each of the four stairs
has 91 steps. This results, together with the
top terrace, in number 365 of the solar
year.

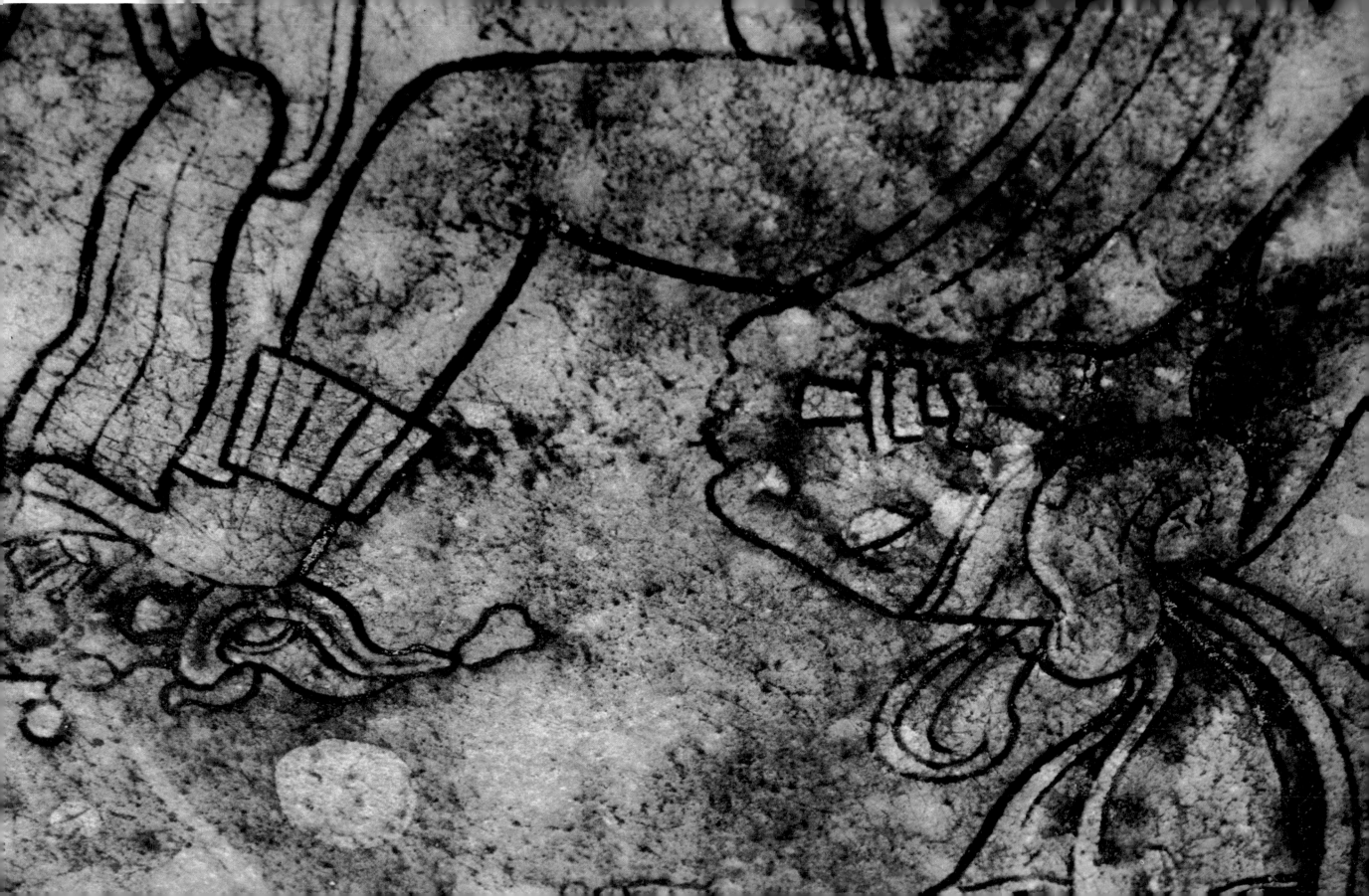

Viva el gran pasado

Explanations of the photos, pages 55 to 66

55 Stone relief on the border of the jungle in Bonampak. Glaring sunlight, which broke through the trees of the virgin forest at the ideal moment, threw this head into relief. There is no way of telling just how long the unprotected stone plates will be able to withstand the strong influences of the weather.

56 Tula is a Mexican town located in the
57 vicinity of the ruins of Tollán. Scientists doubted for a long time that these ruins were actually the relics of the fabulous town which had been the capital of the Toltecs from 856 to 1168 AD. However, when the Mexican archaeologist Jorge R. Acosta began his excavations in 1940, the old legend was confirmed. While the main temple is completely destroyed, the field is dominated now by a five-story temple pyramid with an extended platform. The roof was carried by pillars and telamones, 151/2-ft.-high powerful warrior figures. The structural elements were joined again during the restoration work. The effect was further accentuated by the selection of an unusual angle of exposure.

58 The "Cruciform Temple" in Palenque.
59 Palenque is situated in a jungle-covered chain of calcareous hills, south of the Usumacinta River. The unique spell which surrounds this place is due not only to the fact that the virgin forest forms the very stage of the temple, but also in the graceful design of the buildings. The highest constructions of all the known Maya centers were erected here. And the elaborate stucco technique of wall lining was also applied here. A great surprise was the discovery of a tomb in the interior of the Inscription Temple by Alberto Ruz in 1952. The fact that Palenque was not only a place of sacrifices but also of burials indicates an unexplained correspondence with the ancient Egyptian worship of the dead.

60 If you raise your head at the entrance to
61 the fresco-covered rooms of the temple in Bonampak, you will discover strikingly beautiful cultic and religious representations on the top edge of the entrance. Unfortunately, the tropical humid air has here also gone a long way in its destructive work, and nothing but relics of the former colors have been left.

62 Detail of a rock plate at the foot of the
temple stairs in Bonampak. Here again
one is overwhelmed by the highly artistic
skill. At the same time, it is striking that
here again the various persons are
represented only in profile.

63 Sacrificed and color-treated dead heads
in a wall of Chichén Itzá. Death obviously
had a particular significance with the
Mayas. They confirm the old writings about
human sacrifices having been made in
Chichén Itzá by throwing young women
into the deep waters of the still-existing holy
pond. After many failures, Edward Herbert
Thompson finally succeeded in discovering,
through systematic underwater researches,
several of these human sacrifices.

64 One of the most overwhelming impressions
65 was the moment I climbed the steep stairs
of the Warrior's Temple and suddenly saw
the stone figure of a god called Chac-Mool
by the Mayas. Half-lying, half-rising, Chac-
Mool holds a tray in which the faithful
presumably placed the offerings dedicated
to the gods. Behind, there are two pillars in
the form of rearing snakes whose heads lie
on the floor, while the hook-shaped back-
bent ends of the bodies were designed to
carry the roof. A thick forest of richly
carved columns stands in front of the temple;
this accounts for the often-used name of
"Thousand Column Palace." Nowhere in all
Yucatán is there any other more perfect
construction than this.

66 To conclude the chapter dedicated to the
witnesses of times gone by, a detail picture
from the interior of a temple on Palenque.
Calendar hieroglyphs remind one of all the
research work still required to produce a
truer picture of the magnitude and force
of the old Mexican civilization.

Viva la Santa Virgen

Explanations of the photos, pages 69 to 80

69 In no other country are there as many churches as there are in Mexico. And no wonder that it is so, what with 96% of the population being Catholic. True, the pure-bred Indian tribes have interlaced their old rites and ceremonies with the faith of the Spanish conquerors, but they are nevertheless professed believers in God's Trinity. The church festivals, with their colorful processions, reveal the deep religious urge of the Mexican people. One of the major places of pilgrimage is Guadalupe Hidalgo, a town right in front of Mexico City's gates. This town, where there stood once, long before the Spanish invasion, a temple dedicated to Coatlicue, Goddess of the Earth, is the place where the legend of the Virgen de Guadalupe is said to have taken place. As the legend goes, the Indian Juan Diego was on his way to the church of Tlaltelolco, in 1531, when the Virgin Mary suddenly appeared in front of him on the hill called Tepeyac. She was dark-colored, and commanded him to ask bishop Juan Zumárraga to build a church here, so that she might be close to her people, to love it and protect it. However, the bishop doubted Juan Diego's words and wanted a proof from the heavenly speaker to support his message. She allegedly appeared three times again to her messenger, and as he brought his new report and roses from the Blessed Virgin to the bishop, the portrait of the Holy Virgin, which was to become later the much venerated Virgen de Guadalupe, was impressed on his cloak. On seeing this apparition, the bishop is said to have fallen to his knees and prayed to be forgiven for his doubting. On the 12th of December, the very day on which the image supposedly appeared on the scapulary, Mexico celebrates its most important religious holiday. Thousands of natural flowers are braided into wreaths and symbols and decorate the façade of the basilica.

70 Many pilgrims arrive several days in
71 advance all ready to make their vow: a slow
crawl on their knees over the wide square,
all the way into the church interior up to the
picture of the Holy Virgin.

72 Women wishing for the joys of motherhood
73 are joining the numerous mothers with their
small children in the prayer.

74 The closer the 12th of December gets, more
pilgrim groups come in. Many a pilgrim
spends the night sleeping in the square in
front of the church, while regional dance
teams sing, play and dance.

75 The bright colors of the Mexican people
show up fully: red in an undaunted contrast
with blue, black interfused with white and
neighboring golden ochre.

76 The pilgrims bring along their own altar-
77 piece of the Holy Virgin from their far-away
places to have it blessed in Guadalupe.

78 The sons of the land, one can see them
here as if they were performing on a huge
stage: full of life and style, dressed in the
most flashing colors. Starting with the
Tarahumaras from the ravined mountains
of the Sierra Madre Occidental and up to
the Chamulas from the virgin forests in
Chiapas, they have all found their way here.

79 What a face! It is imprinted both with vigor
and hardness, joy and melancholy!

80 No woman would enter the basilica before
having previously covered her hair with a
cloth. This young girl was strikingly beautiful;
yet, I could find no trace of lipstick or eye
make-up on her face.

DR. DON ART RO VELEZ MAR-
NEZ A LA NION DE DANZA
DI GIDA POR EL CA-
AGUILAR A DEVO-
SAN JOSE PA-
CESIS DE TOLU-
STO 11 DE 1972

Viva la Santa Virgen

Explanations of the photos, pages 83 to 94

83 The freshly blessed communal glass-cases, which shelter the portrait of the Madonna, are brought by the villagers to the waiting wagons. Merry and happy, the whole pilgrim group now proceeds on the journey back home, only to start again someday, on the same road again, when there will be too little left of today's blessing.

84 Teams of amateur artists perform plays dealing with the historical development.

85 One could well imagine this scene transposed back in the year 1810, when the uprising Mexicans attacked the Spaniards, wearing the picture of the Virgen de Guadalupe on their flags. Their leader, Miguel Hidalgo y Costilla, was a village priest in Dolores in what is the Federal State of Guanajuato today. The Spaniards themselves were also marching behind the picture of the Madonna, that of the white-skinned Virgen de los Remedios. The later victory over the Spaniards removed whatever doubt there may have been regarding the wonderful protectress Virgen de Guadalupe. Her picture was sold everywhere, for it is supposed to protect both the owner of a house and the driver of a car. The picture is not missing either from any of the battered country buses, and one can find it even on the bottles of Tequila.

86 This picture as you now see it is reproduced as it was originally photographed. (No trimming was made on any of the other photos either, and the original picture composition was taken as a basis also in this case, the size of the book itself resulting from the proportional correlation of photographs with reproduced pictures.) I wanted to emphasize the situation through the motion of the bodies and their clothes, and nothing else: two different generations are sliding over the wide, hard paving-stone-covered square. And no matter how very much in love the young girls and boys may be, as they swing across the square and approach the center, they will still be looking in the direction of the picture of the Virgen de Guadalupe. And cross themselves, at the same time.

87 This picture clearly suggests the fervor with which this family prays to be heard. The many people about them could never divert them from their prayer: carrying the most beautiful flowers as offerings in their hands, creeping on their knees, they slowly approach the portal to feel at last the rapture of being so close to the Holy Virgin. Mexico is a volcanic country. Earthquakes, typhoons, storm tides, floods, droughts, famine, epidemics – these are still today the ever-present perils on the Indios' way through life, and a prayer could really never harm, particularly when the sky spans so bright blue over the Sierra Madre.

88 On the 12th of December, the Roman Catholic church displays all its splendor – the highest priests bless the immense crowd both within and without the basilica. And indirectly, of course, the millions in front of television screens. For the church of Mexico could hardly miss the opportunity of using the most up-to-date means of communication to influence the consciousness of the people. And distance is certainly a thing of the past: the curious camera scans the Cardinal's face, follows the motions of his hands, fills the screen with the host.

89 Politicians could be jealous: thousands of people converge on this town and crowd the much too small interior of the church, for it could never be compared to the immense cathedrals in Mexico City and Puebla. Both were erected on the exact place where the Temple Pyramids of the Aztecs once stood. One cannot but think of the Aztecan priests who tore out the heart of the human offering through a single quick handling of the obsidian knife. Could the Spaniards, in the presence of these mighty stone-built witnesses of their European civilization, ever drive the memory of the powerful greatness of the Aztecan Empire from their minds?

90
91 Obviously, this day is also an opportunity for dancing and playing. The traditional faces of the liberation wars are being represented in the costumes of their time. Silver Cock and Swords are confronted with the Cross. The popular heroes Hidalgo and José María Morelos are born anew in the play.

92 A group of dancers has come with its own flag and in wonderfully colored garments.

93 The prayer these men are offering could very well be something like this:
All our children, even those living on the border of wilderness,

may their ways lead safely there,
may forests and bushes
stretch out their water-swollen arms
to refresh their hearts;
may their ways lead safely there,
to make them happy, free of hindrances,
may all the boys,
may all the girls,
and those with the sun of life still ahead
of them,
may their hearts be vigorous
and their minds brave.

94 The feast is over, the great occasion is past: now there is nothing left but the long way home. But there is bound to be some solution – there always is one in Mexico, anyway!

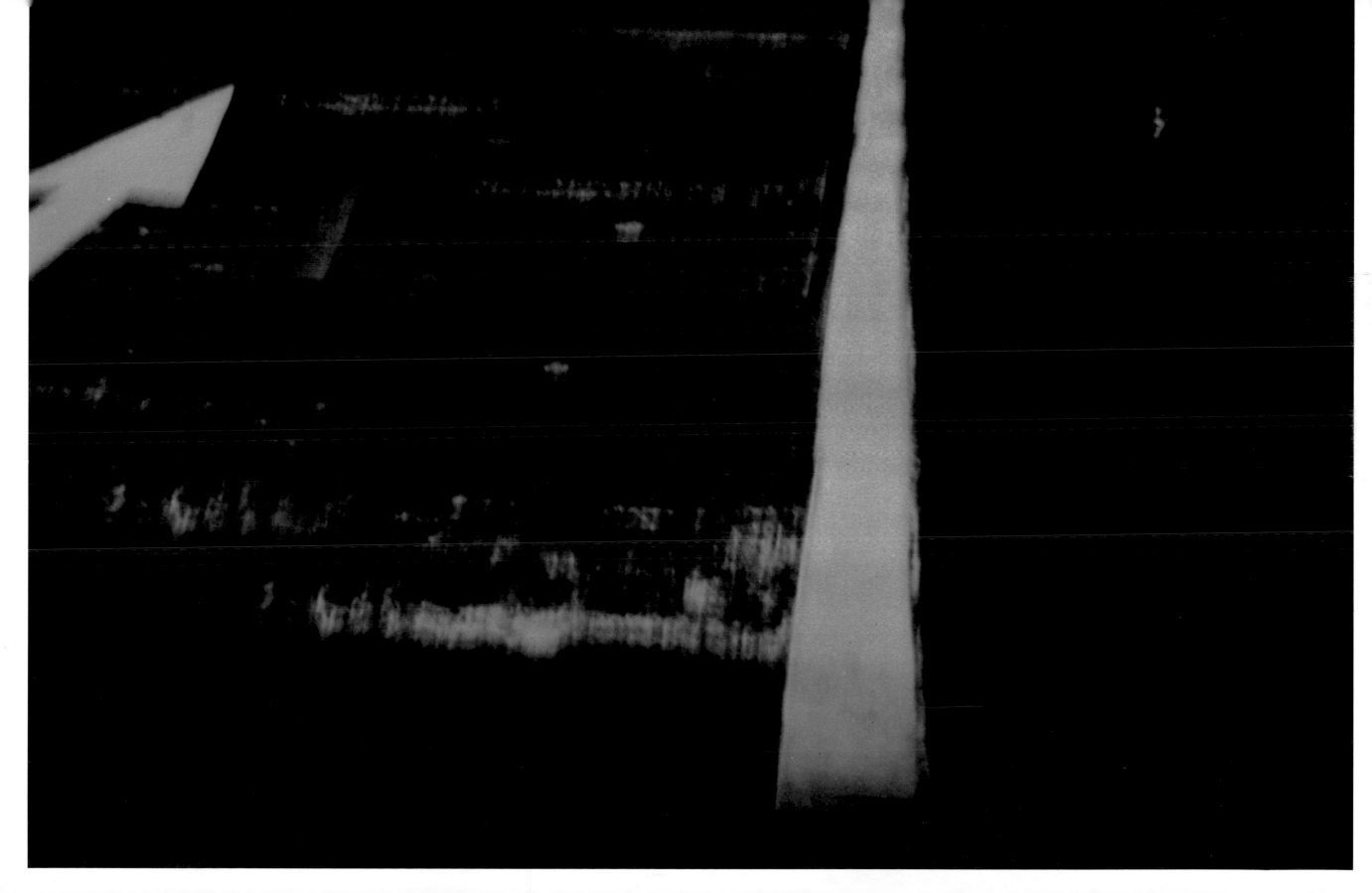

Viva este gran país

Explanations of the photos, pages 97 to 108

97 After having brought to life anew, in the first chapter, the witnesses of times gone by, and dedicated the second chapter to the Festival of the Virgen de Guadalupe (who is said to contribute more to the unity and the understanding of the many families of tribes and languages than all the political efforts), this chapter of the book is intended to emphasize the magnificence of the landscape. In my imagination, Mexico was always a small country. And yet, after Brazil and Argentina, it is the third largest country in Latin America. Just a few figures to size the country up: the border to the north stretches nearly 2,000 miles, to the south some 760 miles, to the east, along the Atlantic Ocean, about 1,720 miles, and to the west, the coast along the Pacific Ocean is not less than 4,470 miles long! The wide highland between the Sierra Madre Occidental and the Sierra Madre Oriental is surpassed in size only by the plateaux in Bolivia and Tibet. Rain-soaked virgin forests, lifeless, dried-out deserts, perpetually snow-covered mountain peaks rising over 16,000 ft. high, or sandy beaches along the ocean front, all this is summarized in just one word: Mexico. And when it comes to the country's capital, nothing but superlatives again: only Moscow's Red Square is larger than the Zócalo, the main square of Mexico City. This is where the cathedral, the continent's biggest, proudly stands.

98
99 Round the Zócalo there is an endless stream of cars driven by wild, resolute drivers and stopped only now and then by the green light for pedestrians.

100 Mexican land: the unmistakable structure of the slopes and valleys, of the trees and beaches. And the charm of restrained colorfulness.

101 To make it easier for the peasants in search of quick help in prayer, a small chapel has been built far away from the village, in the middle of the fields.

102 All day long I had tried to photograph the Popocatépetl, but it was always wrapped up in clouds. Just no luck. Yet in the evening, as I was on my way back to Mexico City, there suddenly developed a strange atmosphere and the sun finally succeeded in breaking through the thick, dark clouds.

103 I first caught a glimpse of the Pico de Orizaba quite early in the morning, when the sun was still dim. Called Citlaltépetl (Star Mountain) by the Indians, the 19,000-ft.-high giant is the country's highest mountain. It forms the eastern corner pillar of the Central Mexican Tableland, which falls away very steeply here towards the tropical lowland and the Gulf of the Caribbean Sea. The southern front of the highland block is crowned by the Cordillera Neovolcánica stretching all the way from the Pico de Orizaba in the East to the Nevado de Colima in the West. This region is of volcanic origin and new eruptions are occurring all the time. The youngest burning volcano is Paricutín, which was formed in 1943. The volcanic region as well as the southern part of Mexico are smitten at irregular intervals by earthquakes of varying intensity. North of the Cordillera Volcánica, however, Mexico is virtually safe from earthquakes of noticeable intensity.

104 Strange rocks of the sea in Cabo San
105 Lucas rise out on the peninsula of California. A most dramatic landscape, indeed!

106 Fishing boats on the Lake Pátzcuaro.
107 The fishermen are building their boats in the traditional canoe style and using butterfly wing fishing nets to catch dace. Early in the the morning they paddle out on the lake, form a circle with their boats, and lower their nets into the water. After a long time, all the butterfly nets are hauled out simultaneously, with the fishermen working all the while on their knees. The lake, with its seven islands, is certainly one of Mexico's most beautiful landscapes. It stretches over 12 miles into a mountainous area. One of the islands, Janitzio, is well known for the yearly festival in commemoration of the dead which is being held here on the 1st and the 2nd of November.

108 Secluded landscape of the Sierra Madre del Sur. On the road to Oaxaca, the scene is changing all the time. Steep mountains turn into flat, gentle hills. Yet the deep effect and the charm of the undisturbed landscape is never lost for a moment.

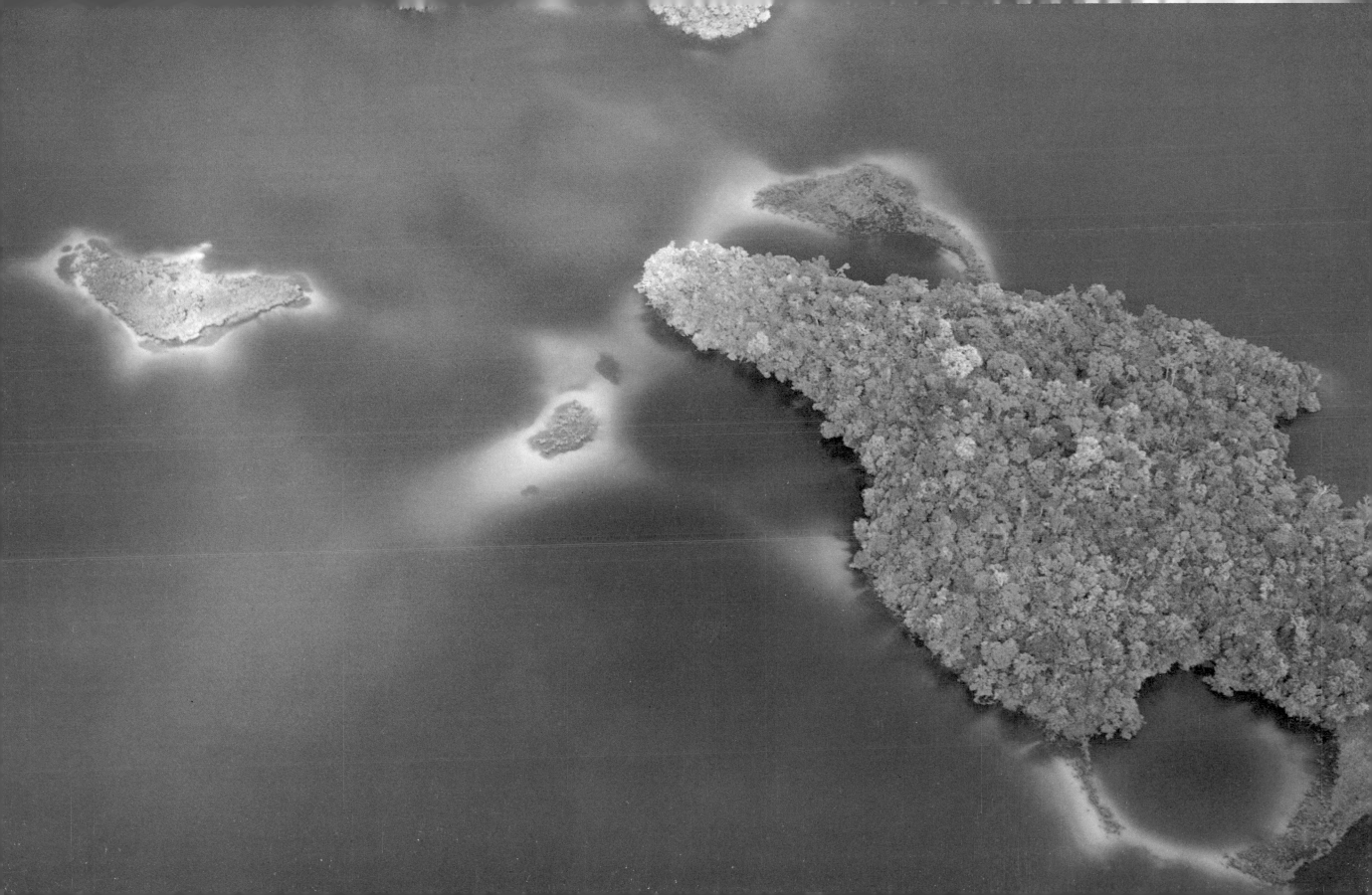

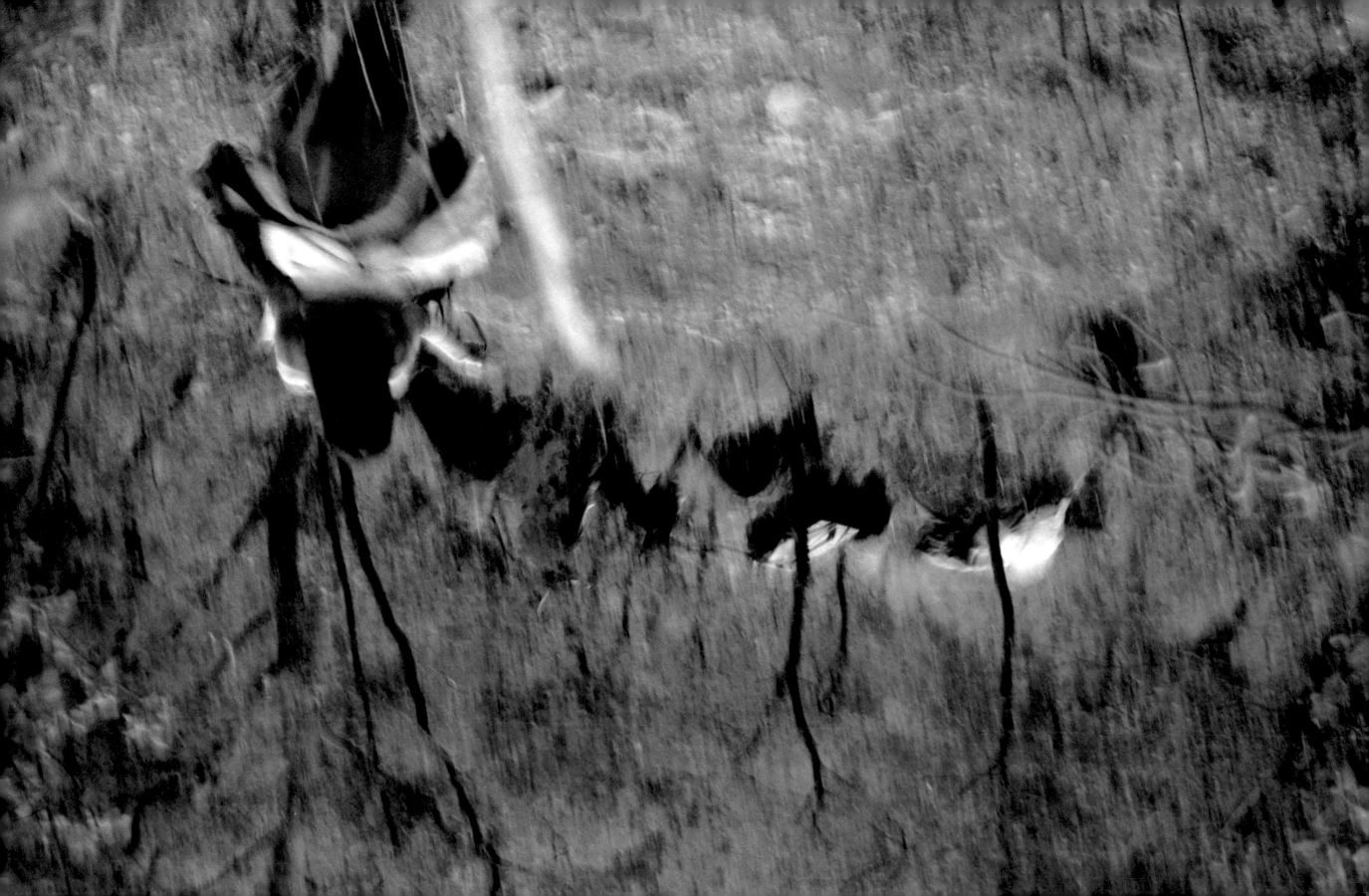

Viva este gran país

111 A lagoon in the Chiapas jungle photographed while on my flight to Bonampak. The thick virgin forest surrounding the territory of the Lacandones can only really be perceived from this height. And one can easily understand why the Spaniards were never able to find these last Mayas, who proudly consider themselves the descendants of the priest kings who could but flee into the inaccessible jungle after their unsuccessful fight against the invaders.

112 In the Gulf of Acapulco. Certainly no other
113 fishing village became as quickly famous and well known as Acapulco. It just has to be in every feature film about the jet-set; and many a thriller novel has been staged there. He who likes amusement and pleasure is sure to find them in numerous fashionable clubs and discotheques; whereas those in search of peace and quietness prefer the bathing bays away from the endless stream of tourists. There is also, of course, a second face to Acapulco, that of the hardworking local population.

114 A diver plunging into the Quebrada.
115 Several times every night, courageous divers jump from a 126-ft.-high rock into the but 17-ft.-wide bay. Hundreds of visitors dining in the restaurants breathlessly watch this unusual spectacle.

116 An expedition to the Rio Urique in the
117 Sierra Tarahumara. Mexico will always linger unforgettably in my memory on account of its wild ravines in the Barranca del Cobre region. I had hired mules and horses to get to the 4,000-ft.-deep canyon to the Rio Urique. It was January. Winter had set in coldly in the mountains. Yet when we reached the river valley, the tropical climate was all about us and we could sleep out of the tents, just in our sleeping-bags, on the warm, bare ground. The river had washed enough branches against the bank to provide us with all the fire-wood we needed.

118 A view of the huge mountain slopes
119 opposite our camp on the first lap of the descent to the Rio Urique. Here live the extremely shy Tarahumaras, famous for their endurance and adroitness in the rocky terrain. This region is one of the last paradises, unaltered and grandiose.

120 Original landscape in Chiapas. The jungle
121 in the Chiapas Mountains is as uniquely
fascinating as the Sierra Tarahumara.
Environmental problems are still a thing of
the future here, nature's basic functions are
still operating faultlessly. But how long will
it stay like this? In Mexico as well, trees are
being felled every day, rocks are being
blasted, and rivers are being diverted in
order to improve communications, to bring
electric power to the villages and the
industries, and to make agricultural
production more economic. And this is
certainly a bold enterprise in a country
where wide dry areas alternate with
massive mountain ranges. The stage of
development in the different parts of the
country varies considerably. All the efforts
at increasing agricultural production in the
northern part of Mexico are hampered by
the still underdeveloped road system.
Only one third of the population in the
north-western part of the country is
supplied with electric power as the
immense distances and the wild, still virgin
nature make power lines an enormously
expensive and difficult achievement.
The same applies to artificial irrigation
works. And yet this is the only way of
making the dry regions of North Mexico
agriculturally useable. Initial irrigation
works had already been made in the
precolonial and colonial periods.
A development program spread over
several decades has yielded already
significant results. It is happening today in
Mexico just as it once happened in Europe
and as it is simultaneously happening in
Africa: the land requires industrial development, and this, in turn, endangers nature's
rhythm.

122 A simple picture of a densely overgrown
mountain slope. Sunbeams are breaking
their way through wonderfully grown trees.
Delicately graded shades of green are the
only colors in this picture. As time goes by,
it will become ever more difficult to

witness nature in such harmonious glory,
free of deformations and of any trace of
human interference.

1872 18 DE JULIO 1972

Viva el mexicano

Explanations of the photos, pages 125 to 136

125 To comprehend the Mexican man one has to realize that many a race has left its mark on his physical and spiritual appearance. Mixtures of Spanish and Indian blood are obviously predominant. The result is difficult to describe: there he is, the merry, ebullient Mexican, singing and dancing, and then, all of a sudden, so full of violence as soon as his honor is endangered. There are a thousand faces to this honor of his: it takes but the innocent declining of his invitation to join him in a glass of tequila to injure it, while any attack on his sister or wife is sure to bring his fear of being dishonored to a climax. "Machismo" ("manhood") is the name given to this particular feature of the Mexican man. Muy macho, to be as manly as possible, this is the absolute ideal (it is, however, too often insufficient). The wrinkled face on the picture at the beginning of the chapter "Viva el mexicano" tells a long story of pride and modesty, fierceness and melancholy.

126 This is what Rosa Elena Luján writes
127 about this picture in her foreword: "It expresses the dignity and kindness of old age." She recognized the essentials at once. How often have these two people been disappointed, how often have they been deceived? Yet nothing could ever affect their confidence in one another.

128 Mothers and fathers with their babies are waiting for admission on the steps of the cathedral in Mexico City. Many parents bring their newborns along to this impressive cathedral to receive benediction.

129 An old woman tries to sell lottery tickets to the man. Playing at lottery is a very popular pastime in Mexico.

130 One of the many colorful markets where you can buy almost anything: cloth, dresses, shoes, knives, jewels, beverages, fruit and animals. A man is trying his luck at playing the organ. He may not get very rich, but somehow or other he does make a living.

131 There's a large supply of high quality, low-priced fruit everywhere. Mexico's generous sun ripens a wide range of tropical fruit: mangos, papayas, melons, figs and many more still. Market-day in the country is always quite an event. Meeting people and gossiping is just as important as buying or exchanging goods. In fact, in spite of the lively currency of coins and notes, one can still see people exchange commodities the way it used to be centuries ago.

132 Market visitors waiting for the bus to take them home. The omnibus, be it for overland trips or just to cover short distances, is Mexico's most common means of transport. There must be thousands of them. The railway system hasn't got very far in this land of wild mountains and ravines. Buses, some of them air-conditioned, connect the various parts of the country. The battered vehicles travelling outside the major towns are always crowded with people, goods and all kinds of animals. And no need to worry about boredom on such a ride, there's laughter, chattering and singing all the time. Most of the drivers could hardly be called anything but adventurous, to say the least.

133 A baby takes the limelight of this picture. It is being admired and entertained. Mexico is a country full of children, families with twelve children are by no means a rarity. In the villages, small children are always carried on the backs of their mothers: it is both practical and supposed to intensify the contact with the mother.

134 The "Floating Gardens" in Xochimilco are
135 a favorite hiking place both for the local population and for the tourists. Hundreds of boats carrying Mariachi players providing for amusement and cheerfulness are moving along the channels. These musical groups usually consist of six men who play merry country music on one or two trumpets, guitars, violins and a bass-guitar. The visitors bring along their lunch and have quite a lot of fun. Particularly suited for lovers. The name "Floating Gardens" refers to the last vestiges of a once widespread system of lagoons, which existed long before the Spanish invasion. The Aztecan town Tenochtitlán was situated in the middle of these verdant, blooming gardens.

136 The simple life of a shepherd – one can still find it in Mexico. This is the great contrast of this country: skyscrapers and palatial bank offices, self-service stores and hotels of international standard in the big cities, simple, primitive life in the country, in the mountains and in the jungle-covered areas.

Viva el mexicano

Explanations of the photos, pages 139 to 150

139 Obviously bored is this young girl as she watches the people on the zebra crossing. She drives a big American car, uses certainly nothing but "sinfully" expensive French cosmetics, and wears only genuine jewels. Has she really anything in common with the cheerful, vigorous women of Yucatán? Does she know her country or just the meeting-points of the rich? For Mexico has its millionaires, too.

140 One of the many policemen who are trying to bring Mexico City's traffic under control. A really insoluble problem. The Mexican temperament manifests itself fully at the steering wheel of a car. Were the streets twice as broad as they are, and the number of thoroughfares still greater than it is, the Mexican at the wheel of his car would have even more opportunities of being "muy macho" – very manly! And thus, there's just one driving duel after another: a risky overtaking maneuver is followed by a quick, cunning lane change, and then again a forceful overtaking. There are few large cities in the world where traffic is as oppressive and hectic as it is in Mexico City.

141 A typical Maya profile encased in the perspex of the protective headpiece. Once again, a comparison with the warrior representations of Bonampak suggests itself quite naturally. Warrior faces of nowadays, armed for the fight in road traffic: wasn't the Mexican Ricardo Rodríguez the greatest Grand Prix driver of all time? And did his premature death in 1962 frighten his brother Pedro in any way? No, he continued racing for another ten years before being killed himself on a high speed course.

142 "Zona Rosa" is the meeting place of the capital's young ones. Here are the boutiques with the craziest dresses. Here are the exclusive cafés and many discotheques, here you can meet the prettiest girls.

143 This impetuous young driver would like nothing better than to sprout wings so that he might overtake the deadlocked cars.

144 Back to the small towns and villages. Here, everything is cosier, calmer, purer and more worth living. I took the picture of the three women, engaged in an impetuous jabber, at the church in Cholula called the "Royal Chapel." It dates back to the 16th century. Like many other churches of the former Toltecan capital, it was built on the foundations of old Mexican temples. From the bell-tower one can see the pilgrimage church Virgen de los Remedios which stands on the highest pyramid of the old Mexican civilization. To avoid any endangering of the pilgrimage church, tunnels are being driven in from below. With its 190,000 sq.yds., this pyramid surpasses Cheops' pyramid in Egypt.

145 Somewhere in Chiapas. Three women with their babies under way. Not a trace of technical interference anywhere – no hurry, no neurosis.

146 Schooling in the open air. This was a rather
147 special experience. Surrounded by a
magnificent landscape, the youngsters
were sitting and lying in the shade of the
trees, with the blackboard standing in the
glaring sunlight in front of them. There was
a lively discussion going on all the time,
not even for a moment were the children
still. When they discovered me (I had
already taken the picture, of course), they
came down upon me with a thousand
questions. As late as 20 years ago, the
number of illiterates was still very high.
However, the introduction of compulsory
education for all children aged 6 to 15 has
done a lot to correct this situation. It is one
of the main tasks the state has got to carry
through. This project takes up almost two
thirds of the national budget, and no
wonder that it is so with some 150,000
communities in the country, of which many
thousands have still no school of their own.

148 Pepsi-Cola and the wide advertisement
boards for this soft drink can be found
even in Mexico's smallest villages.
Mules are often used for the last transport
laps.

149 One of the many stands selling ground-
nuts. It doesn't take very much to make up
the stand: a light table, two or three vessels
for the merchandise, and a couple of
chairs. When the shade of the trees moves
away, so does the whole installation.
"Time is money" is one motto which simply
doesn't apply here. Rather "Mañana," but
mañana could just as well be today or
tomorrow, it goes back into the past and
applies also to the future. Not the same,
however, for those who give up this
peaceful life attracted by the many
temptations of big cities. They have to
change their life completely, they have to
fight much harder than those accustomed
to the ways of life in the city. Young people
are streaming into the city daily, only to
end up, after several false starts,

disappointed, selling chewing-gum, paper
flowers, dolls, newspapers or Kleenex
handkerchieves to smart wholesalers at the
crossings of outlet streets. There is no return,
however, for they would never come back
as failures to their villages. This is how the
slums, or "lost cities," were born, more
miserable than the poorest villages.

150 Rocky habitation of a Tarahumara family
in the Barranca del Cobre region.
Thousands of Indians are still living in this
broken, inaccessible mountainous country,
completely isolated from the civilization of
our day. Radio and television, motor-cars
and electricity are quite unknown.
The Tarahumaras go about barefooted,
hunt with arrows and bows, and catch the
fish in the mountain brooks with nothing
but their hands. Mountain goats and sheep
supply them with milk and cheese. They are
highly superstitious and leave their cave as
soon as one of their family has died there.
Their power of resistance to the hardships
of nature is enormous. They occasionally
still sacrifice animals to their gods.

Vivan los santos

Explanations of the photos, pages 153 to 164

153 With the Lacandones in the jungle of Chiapas. You can fly from San Cristóbal de las Casas to the territory of the Lacandones in a small sporting plane. It is a flight into another world. When you land on the narrow runway funnel which was wrought from the virgin forest, a swarm of curious children surrounds you in no time. I have photographed one of the young girls. Children are the prize treasure of the but 250 surviving Lacandones. Extremely difficult living conditions in the jungle, diseases and poverty account for the few children of the descendants of the Mayas. Intensive welfare measures, and particularly the use of modern medicines, have succeeded in stemming the ever faster dwindling of the Lacandones. The Danish archaeologist Frans Blom and his wife Gertrud have contributed decisively to the survival of this endangered people, and won thereby the deep gratitude and love of the natives. On innumerable occasions they led expeditions on horses and mules to the small, widely scattered villages in the thick jungle to bring help to the local population. In San Cristóbal de las Casas, there is a wonderful house – "Casa Na-Bolom" – half-museum, half caravansary. Ever since Frans Blom's death, his widow has looked after the objects related to the culture and the way of life of the Lacandones, which have been collected over many years.

154 A hearth in one of the primitive huts. Thin
155 wood sticks are being pushed from all around towards the center, where the fire is burning. There is no smoke escape proper, yet the smoke rises readily through the loose wicker-work into the air outside. The everyday pots and pans are mostly burnt black clay utensils. However, visitors and welfare officers have also provided some of the families with a few commodities made of more modern materials.

156 Corn is still the main item of food. But as
157 the gods have to give their blessing to its cultivation, it is being planted only on the days when the moon is in a special position. On the picture, a young girl is picking the corn off the corn-cob; this is turned then into the Indian flour used to bake tortillas. Besides corn, the Lacandones also cultivate beans, tomatoes and tobacco. To hunt birds and animals they use specially treated arrows. The rivers and lakes supply them with fish. And yet, the virgin forest is far from being devoid of perils. There are diseases, such as malaria and yellow fever, and in the water lives the Bilharzia, a tiny parasite which nestles in the human organs, particularly in the liver, and after two years completes its unnoticed destructive work, when the afflicted person can no longer be saved. The contact with foreign visitors is sometimes just as dangerous, more than once did a simple flu kill many a native. Fortunately, a certain adaptation process is currently in progress, and quick-acting medicines prevent disastrous epidemics.

158 Every year, on the 2nd of February,
159 thousands of people go on a pilgrimage
to the Festival of the Holy Virgin in San
Juan de los Lagos. Surrounded by a fore-
court covered with paving-stones, the
mighty church dominates the whole town
from the top of a hill. The festival lasts two
days. Folk-dances and a large and
abundant market ensure a festive
atmosphere. Late in the evening, by the
light of thousands of candles, a solemn
mood seizes all the faithful.

160 The night had been very cold. Early in the
161 morning, small fires began to burn everywhere – on the slopes of the mountains,
on the roadside, in the narrow alleys.
The people were warming their hands at
the fires, and preparing tea or coffee over
them. Later, they formed into groups,
each with its own flag. The procession,
advancing slowly through the steep alleys
towards the church, was spread over
many miles.

163 Like a vision there appeared before us the
163 statue of Jesus the Crucified in the fierce
glaring light of the morning sun.

164 Multifarious were the faces of the natives.
This old woman had the sharp profile of
the Mayas, as we know it from the many
representations handed down over the
centuries.

Vivan los santos

Explanations of the photos, pages 167 to 178

167 The beautiful, energetic face of a young girl amidst the crowd of pilgrims.

168
169 A group of small girls is waiting patiently in the fore-court of the church hoping for an early admission. I was the only photographer to attend this religious festival. No wonder I immediately became conspicuous and was recognized as a foreigner. This explains why on certain pictures of this photographic report, which was made at short time intervals and within a restricted space, some people are looking right at the camera, for they were watching me at work, and understood my intentions quite clearly. However, I never arranged any special grouping of people, nor did I alter any given situation. The selection of the appropriate lens was always the most difficult decision. The use of a panorama-lens, for instance, enabled me to record, beyond the front-row girls, the whole group with their flags, the faces of the men in between, and the façades of the houses.

170 Completely exhausted by the long, wearisome journey, an old man crawls the last yards to the entrance of the church. His feet are tied together, his arms are bound tightly to a wooden frame, which reminds one of a cross. Cactuses with pointed spines are hanging on his breast and back. A crown of thorns is resting on his head. His upper body is bare. On his way, women have spread out their shawls spontaneously to prevent his bare knees from crawling on nothing but the hard ground. Moaning gently, he slowly continues his agonizing advance. A man is fanning him with his hat.

171 Tormented, His forehead bleeding painfully, the suffering figure of Jesus Christ looks out of a glass-case; the glass is spoiled with scratches from the thousands of times it has been touched in awe by the faithful.

172 The old man has reached his objective. After having been lifted over the threshold of the church, he slid the last steps to the altar. What was really the driving force behind this man? Religious fanaticism?

173 The church has filled up, everyone is listening to the sermon. A gentle light has covered all and everything.

174
175 While hundreds of people were crowding into the church, a group was waiting for the priest in front of the gate; he came to bless the flags. Only then did the procession enter the church proper. The flags have been carried right to the front and envelop the altar in bright colors.

176 The festival is over. A woman waits with her two children for the bus to arrive. The journey to the festival was also an opportunity for shopping. A huge market displayed all the goods the countrymen need. The men bought new machetes, the women purchased candles, blankets, shawls and utensils.

177 The same picture one corner farther down the street. From here the buses are leaving for Lagos, León, Silao, Irapuato, Salamanca, Celaya, Querétaro, Guadalajara and other places. The men lean calmly against the wall of the house: the speed and pressure of time is still an unknown concept here.

178 A pair of lovers are completely unaware of the departure. His eyes see nothing but hers. No one could bother them. And neither did I, in spite of my camera and my thoughts coming so close up to them. I was happy just to be able to record on film the gentleness of this moment and made it the closing picture of my photographic report. I may have created, many a time, the impression of stealing with my camera something from the very life and soul of these people. And even though I felt depressed more than once by this thought, I simply couldn't give up my work. The only real justification for it was the awareness of a true and honest representation of this country and its people in the form of this book. And yet, even this book is sure to draw forth the objections of critics. Their reproaches are always the same: "Too much of the unscathed world!" My former book, "Japan – Sunrise Islands," was already, to some critics, an incomplete report on Japan as there was nothing in it on the smog over Tokyo. In fact, whenever I happen to discover nature in all its pure, unaltered splendor in completely out-of-the-way parts of countries like Japan or Mexico, I do not hesitate to give full consideration to this fact in the planning of my book. Everybody knows that there is today smog and garbage in all the big cities. However, few people have ever heard of the last Manchu cranes on Hokkaido or of the Lacandones in the jungle of Chiapas. And if I am given the choice between the simple people in the country and the business-men devoid of any scruples whatsoever in the concrete deserts of the cities, I never hesitate to choose the former. This book is a subjective photographic report on a multilateral country – one part of which I had the opportunity of seeing, and this I am recounting here and now, in my own way. I can only hope that this choice does Mexico justice.

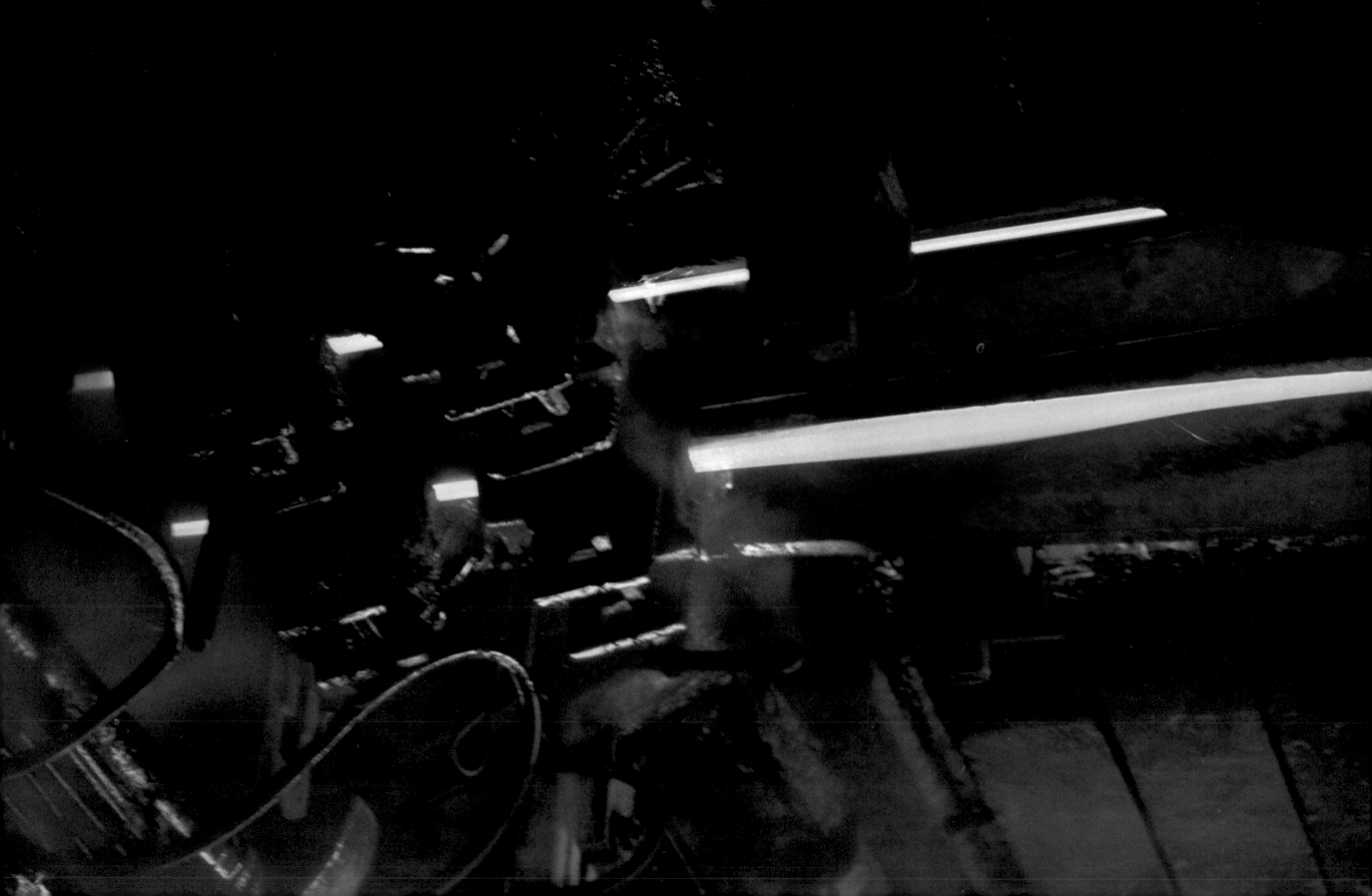

Viva el futuro

Explanations of the photos, pages 181 to 192

181 Mexico is a country rich in natural resources. It is the biggest silver producer in the world and has rich deposits of gold, lead, copper, iron, sulphur and crude oil. The only major coal deposit of the country is in North Coahuila. The coal extracted there is coked in Monclova and then supplied to the steel works in Monclova and Monterrey. The high-grade iron ore, which is mined at Cerro de Mercado, is processed in Monterrey. The oil fields are situated in the country district of Tampico, in the Tuxpán region, and in the southwestern part of Veracruz. The oil industry was nationalized as early as 1938, electricity followed in 1961, and sulphur production in 1967. Among the countries of Latin America, Mexico is one of the most heavily industrialized. Based on the value of the production, the food industry occupies the first place, followed by the textile industry and the iron and steel industry. The center of the heavy industry is Mexico's third largest city, Monterrey, which was founded in 1596. This town was the objective of my visit as I decided to represent the chapter "Industry" in a photographic manner. This synthetic fiber works lies somewhat outside Monterrey, surrounded by strange mountains.
The plant presents a clear architectural arrangement and is equipped with the most up-to-date machines.

182 Thin threads pass through the machine
183 continuously; an operator who is in overall control has sometimes to intervene when some of the threads become entangled.

184 Details of the production process. The
185 threads are wound fully automatically on to spools. The particular color sense of the Mexicans reveals itself here, at the initial point. In the despatch store I saw cloth in bright, gay colors, the kind of colors Mexico's people like and prefer. The color of the clothes and of the houses contribute much to the atmosphere of towns and villages.

186 Surrounded by a forest of spools, the man
187 carries out his work. His main task is one
     of inspection, for the threads are whizzing
     by and winding up on one spool after
     another as if they were driven by an
     unseen hand. Leona Textil is one of the
     major textile fiber producers of the country,
     and its products are of a high quality.

188 Monterrey owes its industrial development
     to its favorable position. Situated close to
     the frontier with the U.S.A., and serviced by the
     main railway line to Central Mexico, the
     town developed rapidly owing to the iron
     ore deposits in the neighboring highland.
     Besides its iron and steel industry,
     Monterrey also accommodates major units
     of the metal, glass, cement and ceramics
     industry. The productivity of the steel
     industry was fully evident at the Hylsa
     Company. Free of any bureaucratic
     complications, I was given every opportu-
     nity of taking pictures, and my impression
     was most positive. I have visited steel works
     in many countries, and Monterrey's
     production shops need not fear any
     comparison. The picture shows an operator
     at a control desk from which he controls
     the rough dressing of the steel blocks.

189 The outer dimensions were also impressive.
     I had to use a car to reach the various
     sections within the works' huge ground.

190 High-grade steel is being cut here into
191 various thicknesses and lengths. This plant
     operates fully automatically.

192 And yet, when it comes to precision opera-
     tions, man is still as indispensable as ever.
     The workers are wearing protective
     headpieces and screens, and when they
     are engaged close to the molten metal
     they put on asbestos suits. Nobody needs
     a match to light a cigarette!

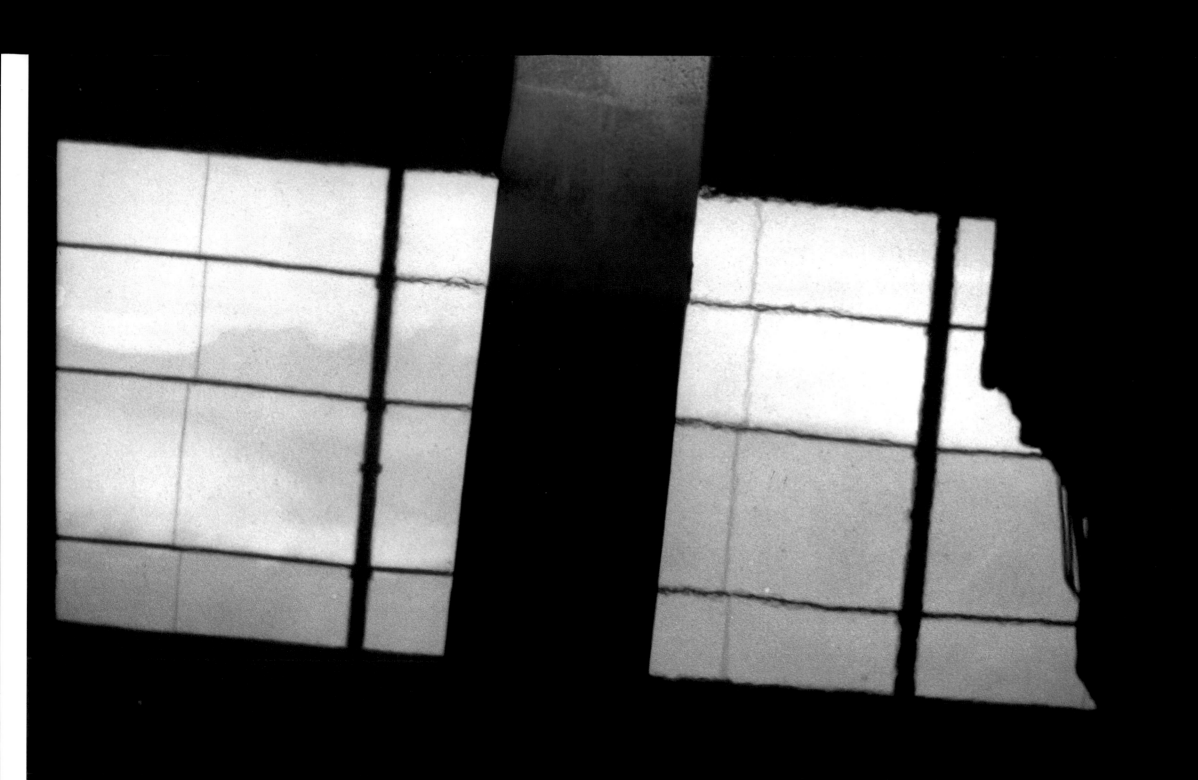

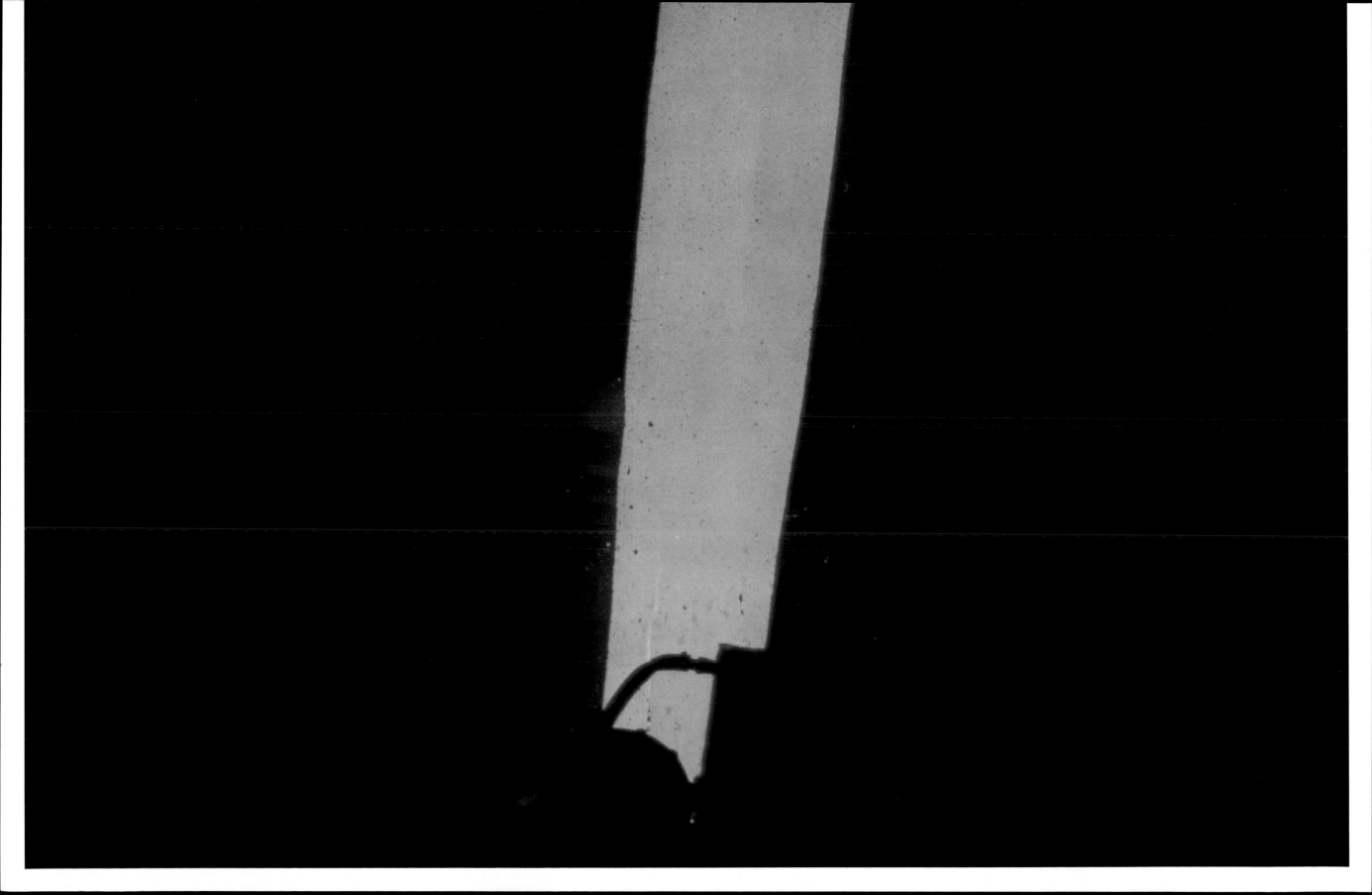

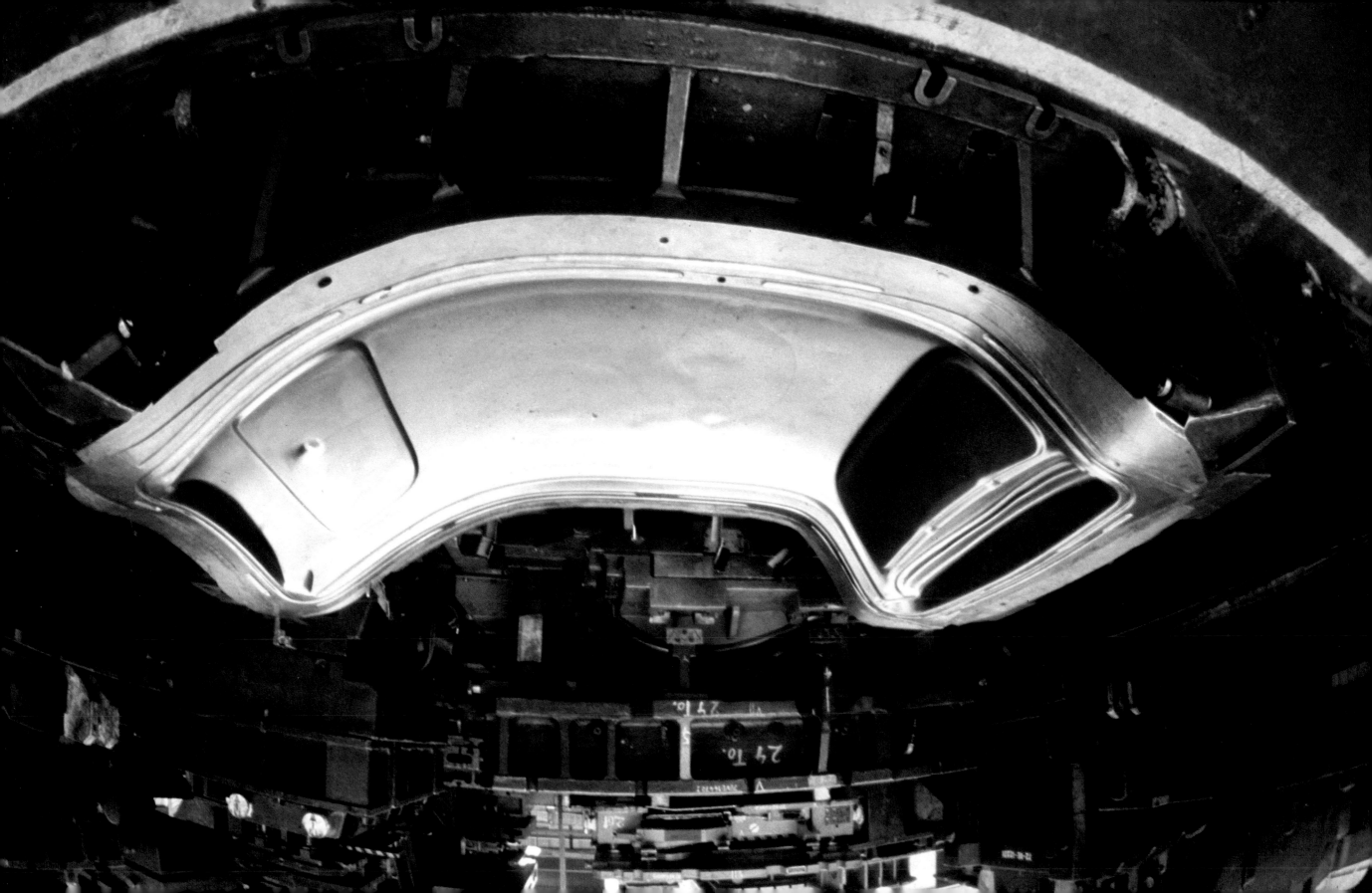

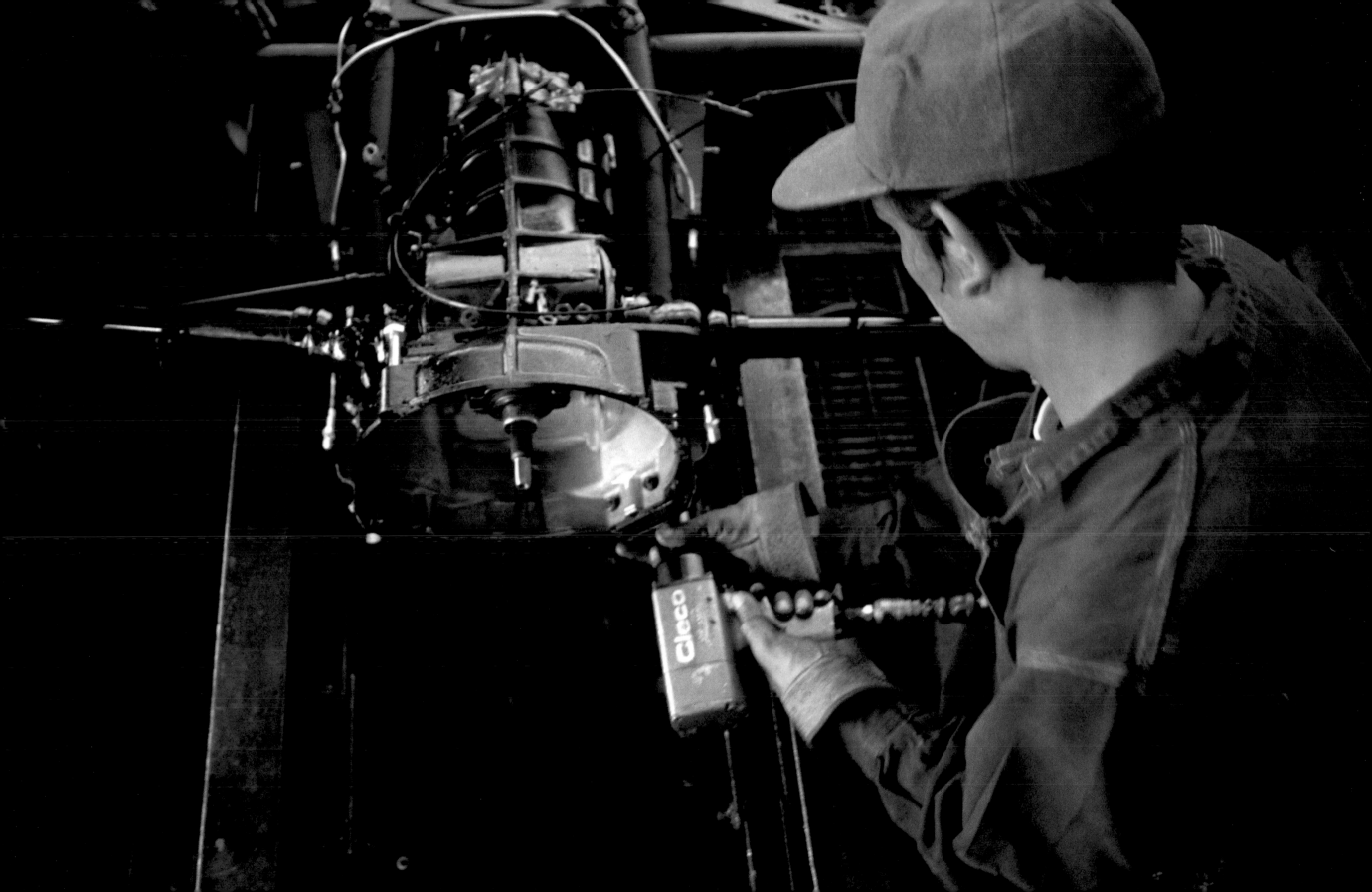

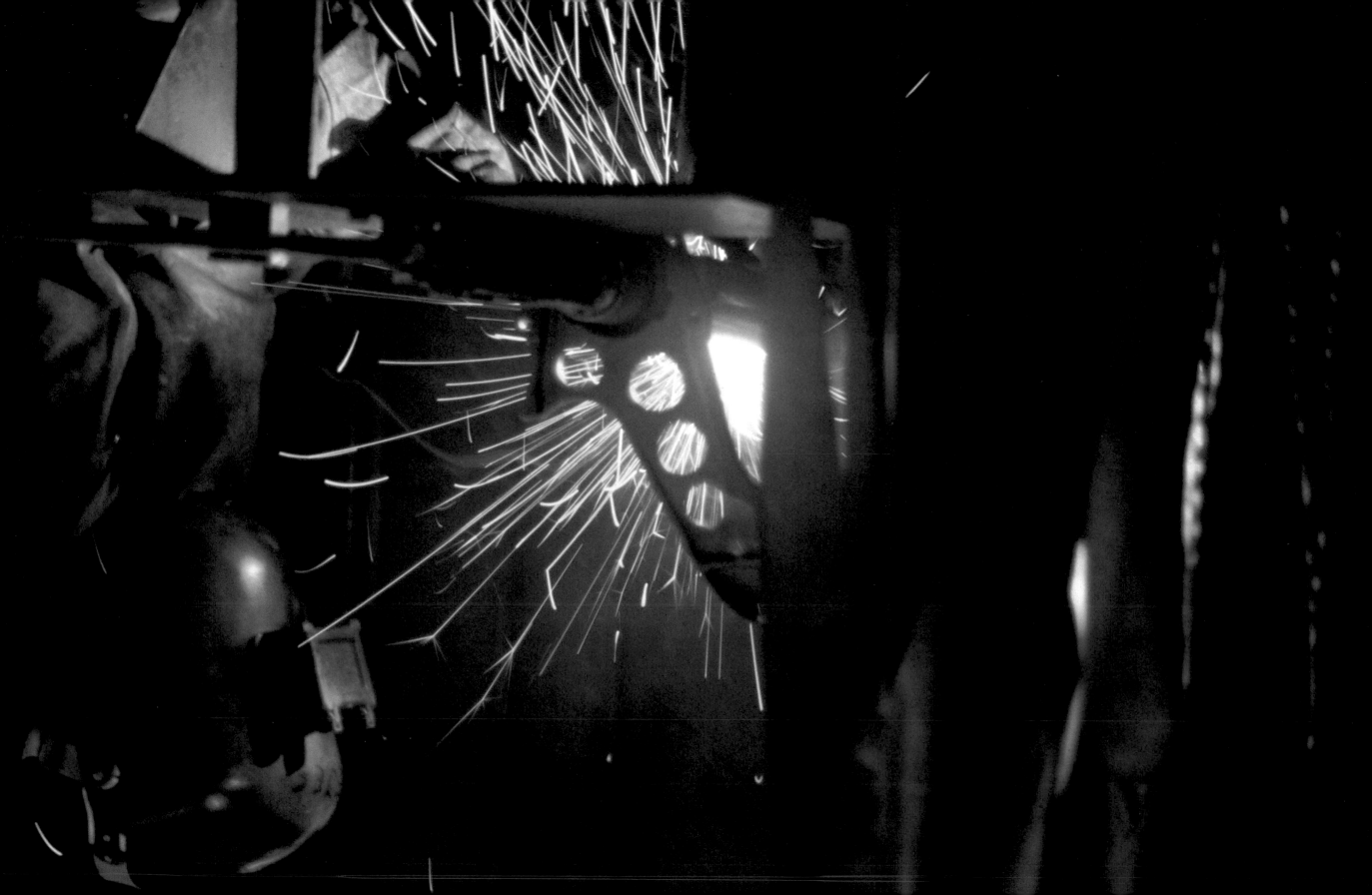

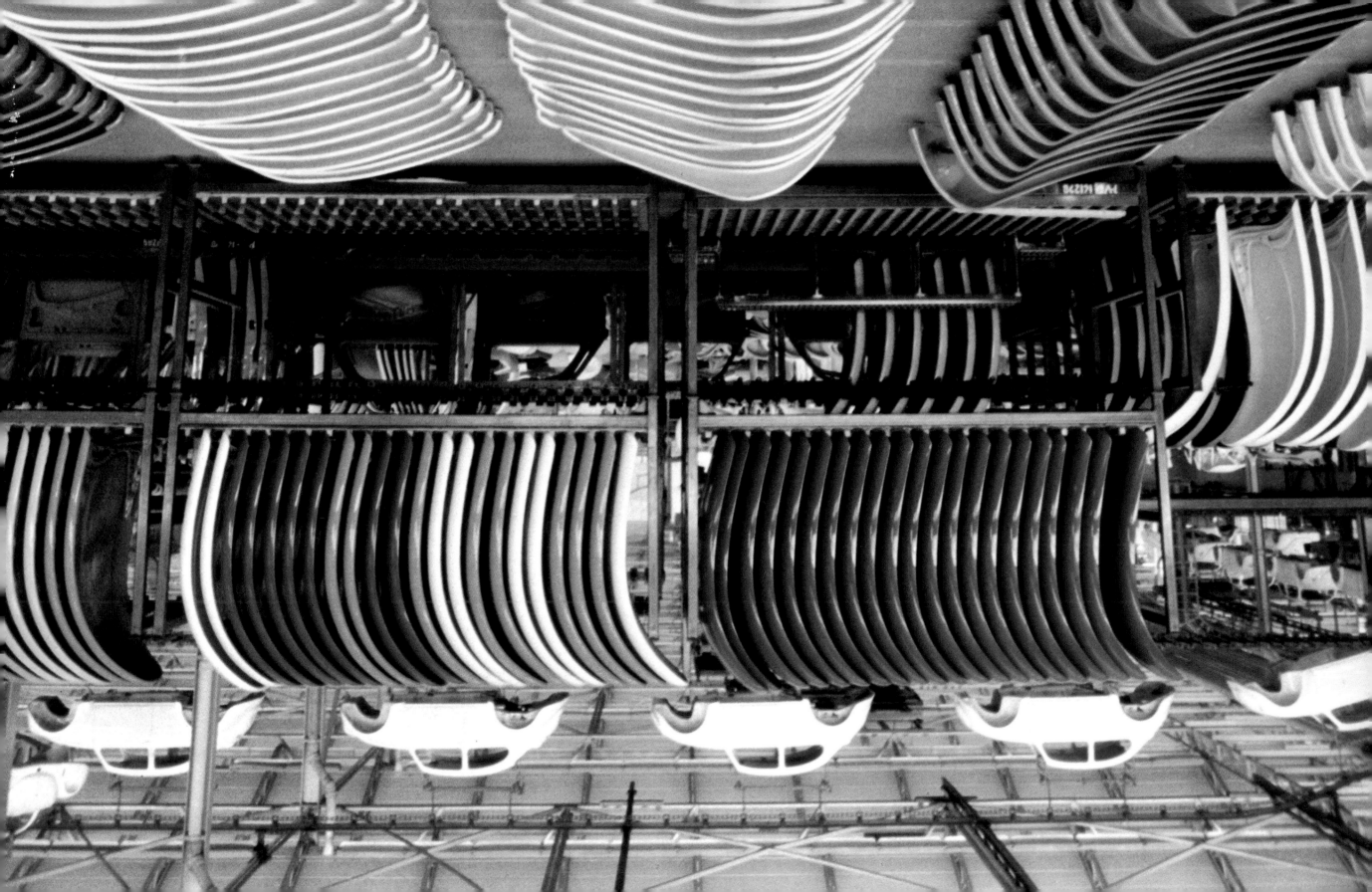

Viva el futuro

Explanations of the photos, pages 195 to 206

195 Surrounded by an intense heat and flying red sparks, the workers, dressed in asbestos suits, tap the molten steel from the furnace. There is only a roof over the plant, no walls, so that the heat may dissipate more rapidly. In spite of the protective clothing, the workers have many singes on their skin. A fresh-air fan supplies cool air.

196 A red-hot steel block is being transferred
197 by crane to the next processing station.

198 Steel blocks from Monterrey may well be used in the Volkswagen Works in Puebla. One cannot but be amazed in front of one of these gigantic presses in which the complete roof of a Volkswagen body is being shaped in a single operation. Both in its details and as a whole, Volkswagen de México is beyond comparison. Here again, I obtained unrestricted permission to take pictures, and working in this immense plant was certainly quite an experience. May I emphasize just a few of the facts I gathered from the documents that were made available to me: Volkswagen de México was established in 1964. The erection work began in Xalostoc, in the vicinity of Mexico City. In compliance with the policy of the Mexican Government of decentralizing the industry, Volkswagen de México decided to build the new plant in the city of Puebla. The decisive factors in selecting the site of the new works were the vicinity of the capital as a major outlet for the plant's products, the possibility of electric power supply from the power plant Malpaso/Tabasco, the existence of a gas long-distance supply pipeline from Minatitlán/Veracruz, as well as the proximity of the port of Veracruz. Furthermore, the region possessed an adequate reserve of labor force. The construction began with the laying of the corner-stone on the 27th of February, 1965. The territory of the works covers an area of some 600 acres, of which 80 acres are of built-up area. There is thus enough ground available for an almost unlimited extension of the production buildings in the future.

199 At the engine and gearing assembly line a worker carries out the operations assigned to him. The average age of the employees is 23, and the majority of them are country people.

200 There is an almost ghostly appearance to this welder dressed in his working-clothes which provide him with adequate protection against eye injuries and burns.

201 And here, in a motor-car production shop, the very quintessence of technical progress, I once again came across a bold profile reminiscent of the faces on the mural paintings and relics of the pre-Spanish days.

202 The availability of unlimited construction
203 ground has made it possible to ensure rational and economic production conditions. The preparation work and the rhythm of the production process feature a rare spirit of exactness. All the Volkswagen branches in the country are characterized by a uniform, unmistakable external aspect and a clear internal arrangement principle, and the plant in Puebla is no exception to this rule. The double color-page gives us a good idea of this. There is little doubt that this industrial unit will lead to the development of other industrial branches. Volkswagen de México's own apprentice workshop enjoys a particular and well-deserved consideration. 300 mechanics and other skilled workers are trained here in each of the three-year courses.

204 At the beginning of 1973, Volkswagen de México was producing various base models, and especially the Volkswagen Safari. It is the first motor-car to be produced completely in Mexico since 1971 and exported to many countries. The picture shows the car's untreated body-works, which receive their actual coatings of paint in the spraying shops after having previously passed through the dipping baths, being transferred on runway rails to the engine and electrical equipment assembly stations.

205 The passage of the sprayed bodies to the various assembling stations is program-controlled. The inspection of the lighting installation and the testing of the engine and brakes are the last operations along the production line.

206 Over the last decades, Mexican artists have called the attention of the people, through grandiose mural paintings, to its history and traditional way of life. The names of José Clemente Orazco, Diego Rivera, David Alfaro Siqueiros and Rufino Tamayo have become very popular. When it comes to the representation of the new realism, one could hardly leave technology out. Thus, the blank steel sheets could very well be part of a huge fresco representing the Mexico of today.